Pattern-Free Fashions

Contemporary Quilting Series

Applique the Ann Boyce Way, by Ann Boyce
Complete Book of Machine Quilting, Second Edition, by Robbie and Tony Fanning
Contemporary Quilting Techniques, by Pat Cairns
Creative Triangles for Quilters, by Janet Elwin
Fast Patch, by Anita Hallock
Fourteen Easy Baby Quilts, by Margaret Dittman
Machine-Quilted Jackets, Vests, and Coats, by Nancy Moore
Pictorial Quilts, by Carolyn Hall
Precision-Pieced Quilts Using the Foundation Method, by Jane Hall and Dixie Haywood
Quick-Quilted Home Decor with Your Bernina, by Jackie Dodson
Quick-Quilted Home Decor With Your Sewing Machine, by Jackie Dodson
The Quilter's Guide to Rotary Cutting, by Donna Poster
Quilts by the Slice, by Beckie Olson
Scrap Quilts Using Fast Patch, by Anita Hallock
Speed-Cut Quilts, by Donna Poster
Stitch 'n' Quilt, by Kathleen Eaton
Super Simple Quilts, by Kathleen Eaton
Teach Yourself Machine Piecing and Quilting, by Debra Wagner
Three-Dimensional Appliqué, by Jodie Davis
Three-Dimensional Pieced Quilts, by Jodie Davis

Creative Machine Arts Series

ABCs of Serging, by Tammy Young and Lori Bottom
The Button Lover's Book, by Marilyn Green
Claire Shaeffer's Fabric Sewing Guide
The Complete Book of Machine Embroidery, by Robbie and Tony Fanning
Craft an Elegant Wedding, by Naomi Baker and Tammy Young
Creative Nurseries Illustrated, by Debra Terry and Juli Plooster
Creative Serging Illustrated, The New, by Pati Palmer, Gail Brown, and Sue Green
Distinctive Serger Gifts and Crafts, by Naomi Baker and Tammy Young
The Fabric Lover's Scrapbook, by Margaret Dittman
Friendship Quilts by Hand and Machine, by Carolyn Vosburg Hall
Gifts Galore, by Jane Warnick and Jackie Dodson
Hold It! How to Sew Bags, Totes, Duffels, Pouches, and More!, by Nancy Restuccia
How to Make Soft Jewelry, by Jackie Dodson
Innovative Serging, by Gail Brown and Tammy Young
Innovative Sewing, by Gail Brown and Tammy Young
Jan Saunders' Wardrobe Quick-Fixes, by Jan Saunders
Owner's Guide to Sewing Machines, Sergers, and Knitting Machines, by Gale Grigg Hazen
Petite Pizzazz, by Barb Griffin
Putting on the Glitz, by Sandra L. Hatch and Ann Boyce
Second Stitches, by Susan D. Parker
Serge a Simple Project, by Tammy Young and Naomi Baker
Serge Something Super for Your Kids, by Cindy Cummins
Serged Garments in Minutes, by Tammy Young and Naomi Baker
Sew Sensational Gifts, by Naomi Baker and Tammy Young
Sew, Serge, Press, by Jan Saunders
Sewing and Collecting Vintage Fashions, by Eileen MacIntosh
Simply Serge Any Fabric, by Naomi Baker and Tammy Young
Soft Gardens, by Yvonne Perez-Collins
Stretch & Sew Guide to Sewing on Knits, by Ann Person
Twenty Easy Machine-Made Rugs, by Jackie Dodson

Open Chain Books

Gail Brown's All-New Instant Interiors, by Gail Brown
Jane Asher's Costume Book, by Jane Asher
Learn Bearmaking, by Judi Maddigan
Quick Napkin Creations, by Gail Brown
Sew Any Patch Pocket, by Claire Shaeffer
Singer Instructions for Art Embroidery and Lace Work
Soft Toys for Babies, by Judi Maddigan

Crafts Kaleidoscope

The Banner Book, by Ruth Ann Lowery
Crafter's Guide to Glues, by Tammy Young
Creating and Crafting Dolls, by Eloise Piper and Mary Dilligan
Daddy's Ties, by Shirley Botsford
Fabric Painting Made Easy, by Nancy Ward
How to Make Cloth Books for Children, by Anne Pellowski
Quick and Easy Ways With Ribbon, by Ceci Johnson
Stamping Made Easy, by Nancy Ward
Too Hot to Handle?/Potholders and How to Make Them, by Doris Hoover

StarWear

Embellishments, by Linda Fry Kenzle
Make It Your Own, by Lori Bottom and Ronda Chaney
Mary Mulari's Clothing With Style, by Mary Mulari
Pattern-Free Fashions, by Mary Lee Trees Cole
Shirley Adams' Belt Bazaar, by Shirley Adams
Sweatshirts With Style, by Mary Mulari

Know Your Sewing Machine Series, by Jackie Dodson

Know Your Bernina, Second Edition
Know Your Brother, with Jane Warnick
Know Your Elna, with Carol Ahles
Know Your New Home, with Judi Cull and Vicki Lynn Hastings
Know Your Pfaff, with Audrey Griese
Know Your Sewing Machine
Know Your Singer
Know Your Viking, with Jan Saunders
Know Your White, with Jan Saunders

Know Your Serger Series, by Tammy Young and Naomi Baker

Know Your baby lock
Know Your Pfaff Hobbylock
Know Your Serger
Know Your White Superlock

Teach Yourself to Sew Better Series, by Jan Saunders

A Step-by-Step Guide to Your Bernina
A Step-by-Step Guide to Your New Home
A Step-by-Step Guide to Your Sewing Machine
A Step-by-Step Guide to Your Viking

Pattern-Free Fashions

12 Easy Styles to Sew • Serge • Fuse

Mary Lee Trees Cole

Chilton Book Company
Radnor, Pennsylvania

DEDICATION:

*To the women of my family
who passed down a love of creating with fabric,
and to David and Aaron.*

ACKNOWLEDGEMENTS:

*I would like to thank Robbie Fanning for encouraging me to undertake this book
and put my ideas in print, and Rosalie Cooke for her hours of careful editing.
I would also like to thank Joy Stocksdale for her encouragement and help
(her handpainted silk vest is featured on the cover),
and my friend Arlene Dunn, who shared her sewing expertise.*

Designed by Heather McLaren

Edited by Robbie Fanning and Rosalie Cooke

Produced by Rosalie Cooke

Cover photo by Mark Jenkins

Interior photos by Lee Lindeman

Illustrations by Deva

Manufactured in the United States of America

Cover
*Left: Hand painted vest by Joy Stocksdale, 2145 Oregon Street,
  Berkeley CA, 94705. Belt created by Ellen Edith, Box 646,
  Boulder Creek CA, 95006.*
*Classic blouse (Chapter Three) and pants (Chapter Ten)
  of polyester*
*Center: Classic blouse (Chapter Three) in linen and skirt
  (Chapter Four) in silk*
*Right: Timeless top (Chapter One) in satin acetate, sarong
  skirt (Chapter Twelve) and cocoon (Chapter Thirteen) in
  sandwashed silk*

Library of Congress
Cataloging-in-Publication Data

Cole, Mary Lee Trees.

Pattern-free fashions: 12 easy styles to sew, serge, fuse/

p. cm. — (StarWear)

Includes bibliographical references and index.

ISBN 0-8019-8497-1 (pb)

1. Costume design. 2. Dressmaking.
I. Title. II. Series.

TT507.T83 1995   94-23897 CIP

646.4'04—dc20

1234567890 432198765

Contents

FOREWORD vii

CHAPTER ONE: GET READY, GET SET. 1
Get Ready, Get Set . . . For Unusual
  Designs That Flatter 1
Get Ready, Get Set . . . To Sew–Serge–Fuse . . 1
Get Ready, Get Set . . . With Supplies 2
Get Ready, Get Set . . . To Get
  Measurements 2
Get Ready, Get Set . . . For Patterns Made
  of Squares and Rectangles 4
Get Ready, Get Set . . . To Prepare Your
  Fashion Fabric For Cutting 5
Get Ready, Get Set . . . To Fuse Garments
  Together 6
Get Ready, Get Set . . . For Easy Ways
  To Make Clothes Fit 7
Get Ready, Get Set . . . To Have Fun
  Embellishing Your Garments 10
Get Ready, Get Set . . . GO! 13

CHAPTER TWO: TIMELESS TOP 15
Projects 15
Tips for Planning Your Top 15
What to Buy 16
Prepare Your Fabric 16
Create Timeless Top Pattern
  and Cut Fabric 16
Construct Your Top by Sewing 17
Construct Your Top by Serging 18
Construct Your Top by Fusing 18
Finishing Touches 19

**CHAPTER THREE: CLASSIC BLOUSE
  & TURTLENECK TOP** 21
Projects 21
Tips for Planning Your Classic Blouse
  or Turtleneck Top 21
What to Buy 21
Prepare Your Fabric 21
Create Blouse or Turtleneck Pattern
  and Cut Fabric 22

Construct Your Classic Blouse 24
Construct Your Turtleneck 25
Finishing Touches 25

CHAPTER FOUR: GATHERED SKIRT 27
Tips for Planning Your Skirt 27
Projects 27
What to Buy 27
Prepare Your Fabric 28
Create Gathered Skirt Pattern Shapes
  and Cut Fabric 28
Construct Your Simple Gathered Skirt 29
Construct Your Simple Straight Skirt 30
Finishing Touches 31

**CHAPTER FIVE: SIMPLEST DRESS
  & JUMPER** 33
Projects 33
Tips for Planning Your Dress or Jumper . . . 33
What to Buy 33
Prepare Your Fabric 34
Create Dress/Jumper Pattern Shapes
  and Cut Fabric 34
Construct Your Dress/Jumper 37
Finishing Touches 37

CHAPTER SIX: SWIRLING GOWN 39
Projects 39
Tips for Planning Your Swirling Gown 39
What to Buy 39
Prepare Your Fabric 39
Create Gown Pattern Pieces
  and Cut Fabric 40
Construct Your Swirling Gown 41
Finishing Touches 43

**CHAPTER SEVEN: CAFTAN ROBE
  & DRESS** 45
Projects 45
Tips for Planning Your Caftan 45
What to Buy 45
Prepare Your Fabric 46

Create Caftan Pattern Pieces
and Cut Fabric 46
Construct Your Caftan Robe or Dress 48
Finishing Touches 49

**CHAPTER EIGHT: EASIEST WINTER COAT
& SUMMER WRAP** 51
Projects 51
Tips for Planning Your Wrap 51
What to Buy 51
Prepare Your Fabric 52
Create Coat and Wrap Pattern Pieces
and Cut Fabric 52
Construct Your Coat or Wrap 54
Finishing Touches 55

CHAPTER NINE: ONE-HOUR VEST 57
Projects 57
Tips for Planning Your Vest 57
What to Buy 57
Prepare Your Fabric 57
Create Vest Pattern Pieces and Cut Fabric . . 58
Construct Your One-Hour Vest 59
Finishing Touches 61

**CHAPTER TEN: SURE-FIT PANTS
& SHORTS** 63
Projects 63
Tips for Planning Your Pants or Shorts 63
What to Buy 64
Prepare Your Fabric 64
Create Pants/Shorts Pattern
and Cut Fabric 64
Construct Your Sure-Fit Pants or Shorts . . . 66
Finishing Touches 67

CHAPTER ELEVEN: KIMONO COAT 69
Projects 69
Tips for Planning Your Kimono 69
What to Buy 69
Prepare Your Fabric 71
Create Kimono Pattern and Cut Fabric . . . 71
Construct Your Unlined Kimono 72
Construct Your Lined Kimono 73
Finishing Touches 73

CHAPTER TWELVE: SARONG SKIRT 75
Projects 75
Tips for Planning Your Sarong 75
What to Buy 75
Prepare Your Fabric 75
Create Sarong Pattern and Cut Fabric 75
Construct Your Sarong 77
Finishing Touches 79

CHAPTER THIRTEEN: COCOON WRAP 81
Projects 81
Tips for Planning Your Cocoon 81
What to Buy 81
Prepare Your Fabric 82
Create Cocoon Pattern and Cut Fabric 82
Construct Your Unlined Cocoon 84
Construct Your Lined Cocoon 85
Finishing Touches 85

RESOURCES 86
Books 86
Periodicals 86
Mail-Order Sources 87

INDEX 88

FOREWORD BY ROBBIE FANNING, SERIES EDITOR

The mail-order catalogs now are full of glamorous wool capes and silk kimonos, all at preposterous prices. I look at them and think, "I could make that tonight, with better fabric for a third of the price." They're nothing but basic manipulated shapes with an opening. Still, some measurements are needed to draft even simple garments and I'm short on time. That's why I'm glad to see this new book by Mary Lee Trees Cole. She's done the calculating for me.

The beauty of using simple squares and rectangles to shape wonderful fabric is that you can do as much or as little as you have time and skills. If you're going to the party tonight, use fabulous fabric—and glue it. If you have a bit more time, try out the decorative stitches on your new sewing machine by using them around the neckline or on top of the shaping pleats.

If ever you needed permission to collect gorgeous, flowing fabric, this book is it. As I handled Mary Lee's garments for the color pages, I found myself burying my face in the sueded rayon, silk noil, handkerchief linen, and velvet.

While it's easy to drape these garments on your own body, it's easier to drape them on a dress form. I recommend buying even a cheap used one and padding it out to your shape. Then it's fun to pinch, tuck, gather, and pleat to your heart's content.

Overleaf:
Bottom left corner: Detail of vest front with button and
  ribbon closures, Guatemalan cotton cloth with knotted yarns
  (Style #4 in Chapter Nine)
Bottom right corner: Detail of Stitch & Stretch®
  gathering tape
Upper left corner: Examples of neckline sketches to try
Center: Examples of tools, threads, glues, tapes, and supplies
  to have on hand

Get Ready, Get Set...

GET READY, GET SET . . .
FOR UNUSUAL DESIGNS THAT FLATTER

When I was creating art-to-wear fashion, I was always on the lookout for good designs. I discovered I wasn't alone in my search. For 5000 years people have been creating garments out of cloth. For centuries, and even today in some cultures, the loom size determined clothing styles. The fabric was not cut when it came off the loom, just draped around the body and simply sewn or laced together with thread, yarn, or leather, and closed with buttons or other fasteners. The "patterns" that evolved were based on squares or rectangles made from one piece of fabric, or several pieces of fabric, with openings for the head, arms, and legs. After hundreds of years of making these garments for men, women, and children of every size and shape, traditional cultures perfected their "pattern-free" designs.

You don't have to use handwoven fabric to create one of these striking, beautiful designs. The projects featured in this book show you how to combine simple shapes cut from commercial fabric of any width into a garment that looks gorgeous on you and is comfortable to wear. If you want, you can draw the squares and rectangles that make up the garment directly onto your fabric with chalk. However, since you'll want to use these designs more than once, I recommend tracing the simple shapes on paper so you can use them again and again. These "patterns" do not have a commercial pattern's close sizing, curves, darts, notches, or gussets, which is another reason I call them "pattern–free."

You'll find style variations inspired by Mexican ponchos, Latin American ruanas, Indonesian jackets, Japanese kimonos, Balinese trousers, and African caftans. Handweavers, fabric artists, and couturier designers use these designs season after season, because they flatter many body shapes and provide the perfect lines for displaying special fabrics and embellishments. Now you too can have fun playing and creating with these twelve easy-to-make styles.

There are many other exciting designs that didn't fit these limited pages. If you're interested in seeing more, check out one of the costume history books in the Resource List and create your own variation. For now, have fun making fashions that fit and flatter with these twelve sew–serge–fuse projects.

GET READY, GET SET . . .
TO SEW–SERGE–FUSE

Many of the projects in this book are so simple you can serge, sew, or sometimes even fuse them together in an hour or two. Their simplicity makes them good projects for beginners. Experienced sewers, crafters, and fabric artists will enjoy creating these fashions with more challenging, unusual fabrics and decorative embellishments.

At the end of the book you'll find an extensive Resource List. It gives sources for finding all the products used in this book. It also tells you where to get help if you're stuck with a sewing, serging, or fusing problem. The focus of this book is to provide "patternless patterns," to introduce fusing techniques, and to give you the basics of putting together these garments. For more detailed sewing and serging instruction, turn to the wonderful reference books listed in the Resource List.

GET READY, GET SET . . . WITH SUPPLIES

Patternmaking Supplies

◆ Paper for making a pattern: tissue paper, butcher paper, or large paper bags (cut open). Avoid newsprint since ink can rub off on your fabrics.

◆ Pencils for drawing patterns on paper: use soft lead like a #2

◆ Large eraser for erasing pencil marks on paper

◆ Straight edge: ruler, yardstick, or grid ruler used for rotary cutting

◆ Right angle: t-square ruler for creating right angles. You can also use the corner of a large manila envelope, a file folder, or a book.

◆ Plate or dish for creating curves at the neckline

◆ Tailor's chalk or non-permanent fabric marking pencils

◆ Measuring tape

◆ Scissors to cut paper pattern

Other Supplies

◆ Scissors or rotary cutter and mat to cut fabric

◆ Sewing pins, needles

◆ Thread: sewing and decorative (optional)

◆ 3/8" (1cm) paper-backed fusible tape (optional)

◆ Fabric glue (optional)

◆ Seam sealant, like Fray Check® (optional)

◆ Elastic: elastic gathering tape (optional), non-roll waistband elastic (optional), regular, soft elastic (optional)

◆ Velcro® hook and loop tape

◆ Embellishments such as braid, binding, trims, ribbons, beads, buttons, appliqués, paints and stencils

GET READY, GET SET . . . TO GET MEASUREMENTS

To get the best fit, you need accurate body measurements. The illustration shows where to measure.

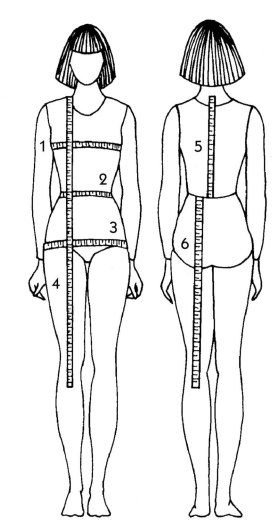

1. Bust
2. Waist
3. Hips
4. Shoulder to hem
5. Neck to waist
6. Waist to hem

Take your measurements.

Referring to your body measurements, use the largest measurement, whether bust or hip, to select your basic garment size from the following:

	Child	Adult Size: 1	2	3	4
Bust	26-29" (66-74cm)	30-33" (76-84cm)	34-38" (85-97cm)	39-42" (98-107cm)	43-48" (108-121cm)
Waist	23-26" (59-66cm)	24-26" (61-66cm)	27-28" (67-71cm)	29-30" (72-76cm)	31" + (77cm +)
Hips	27-30" (69-76cm)	33-36" (84-92cm)	37-40" (93-102cm)	41-44" (103-112cm)	45-48" (113-122cm)

♦ ♦ ♦ i d e a s ♦ ♦ ♦

◆ Take the measurements of everyone you make garments for and keep them on the form which you can photocopy. If you want to make one of the projects for a gift or as a surprise, you'll have the information you need at hand.

Name: Measurements:

	Bust/chest	Waist	Hip	Shoulder to hem	Neck to waist	Waist to hem

_____

_____

_____

_____

_____

_____

_____

_____

_____

_____

_____

Sewing pattern-free garments is not like tailoring a jacket. You have much more freedom in fitting. Therefore, choosing the size to sew is easy. Take your largest measurement and compare it to the chart above. If, for example, your hips are 45" (1.1m), sew a size 4 and control any extra fabric with tucks, pleats, and gathers (explained later in this chapter).

Most of the layouts in this book show measurements for a size 2. Each adult size on the chart is 4" (10cm) bigger or smaller than its neighbor. To change the measurements for your size, enlarge or reduce the width of the basic rectangle by a multiple of 4" (10cm). For example, if you are a size 4, add 8" (20cm) to the total circumference of the size 2 measurements given in the layout.

To determine how much to add at each side, divide the extra inches you need by the number of cut edges. If the garment has side seams and you need 8" (20cm), divide 8" (20cm) by four cut edges. Thus you will add 2" (5cm) at each side seam.

Don't change the size of the neck opening, the armholes, or the sleeves unless you want to for design purposes.

If you need a size larger than shown, first make a paper pattern for size 4 and try it on. These garments are roomy and you may be pleased with that size. If not, add multiples of 4" in total circumference until the garment fits.

Remember, it's easy to enlarge or reduce, shorten or lengthen these shapes, since they are squares and rectangles. Try them out on your body in paper first, if you are uncertain about how loose or tight a garment will be.

GET READY, GET SET . . . FOR PATTERNS MADE OF SQUARES AND RECTANGLES

Every garment in this book is made from simple rectangles. The dimensions for the parts of each garment are in the illustrations. Experienced sewers can try drawing these measurements directly on their fabric with tailor's chalk and a ruler. Another option is to measure and cut the garment pieces with a rotary cutter, using a mat and grid ruler. But if you want to make a design more than once, I recommend that you draw the simple garment shapes on paper so you can use them again and again. I also suggest that inexperienced sewers work the shapes out on paper before they cut into their fabric.

Here's how to make the shapes you will need:

1 Use tracing paper, waxed or tissue paper, brown wrapping paper, or even a brown paper bag. You'll also need pencils and an eraser, nonpermanent fabric marking pencils or tailor's chalk, a measuring tape, and a straight edge ruler or yardstick.

2 Measure and draw your pattern pieces exactly as shown, except to full size.

NOTE: All pattern pieces in this book include a 1/2" (1.3 cm) seam allowance *unless otherwise indicated.*

3 Add or subtract the correct amount for your size from the width or length of the pattern shapes (see page 3).

4 Measure and mark all points with alphabet letters.

5 Cut out the pattern and hold the pieces in place against your body. Look in a mirror to make sure the armhole openings, neck opening, and length of sleeves (if any) and hem are where you want them. Mark any adjustments. If you need to make changes, cut the pattern pieces smaller, or add to them by taping on extra paper.

6 It's fun to draw and cut several necklines to choose from—round, V, U-shaped, or whatever your favorite happens to be. See the illustration for ideas.

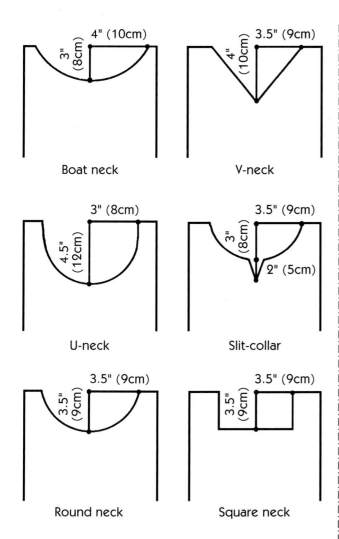

Try different necklines.

First make test samples. Fold a letter-size sheet of paper in half, horizontally. Use a pencil and ruler to measure and draw one-half the neckline shape on the folded edge (like cutting paper valentines or snowflakes). Open up your fold and "try on" the neckline in front of a mirror. To make changes, re-fold the paper and mark your changes in pencil before cutting. To get a round neck, a U-neck, or a boat neck, try using a dinner or salad plate to get the curve you want.

7 Cut the neckline sample along the final lines. "Try on" the pattern pieces you've just made for a final fit. When they're the way you want them, lay them on the garment pattern at the

neckline edge, matching points A (the shoulder line) and points E (the center front and back). You can pin the paper patterns together, which makes it easy to interchange several necklines on the same bodice.

8 Pin the garment pattern on the fashion fabric and cut the fabric along the outside edge of the paper shapes. You can also weigh the pattern down and use a rotary cutter and mat.

9 Use a fabric marker or tailor's chalk to mark the alphabet points on the fashion fabric.

10 Glue, serge, or sew following the instructions outlined in each chapter for constructing the garment.

GET READY, GET SET . . . TO PREPARE YOUR FASHION FABRIC FOR CUTTING

Preshrink fabric to remove excess finishes and to relax it. If your fabric needs to be drycleaned, take it to a dry-cleaner who will charge you a bulk rate, by weight.

If your fabric is delicate, soak for several minutes in a basin of water at whatever temperature you will be using to launder it. Line dry or machine dry, again treating the fabric as you will when you launder it. If you are not going to paint embellishments, add fabric softener to your washer or dryer when you prewash the fabric to eliminate static electricity.

After your fabric is dry, straighten fabric ends to coincide with crosswise threads. If necessary, straighten grain of fabric by pressing with a steam iron or by pulling fabric gently but firmly in the opposite direction from the way the ends slant.

If you're working with a knit fabric, square the ends with the corner edges of a rectangular table or the mat on your cutting board.

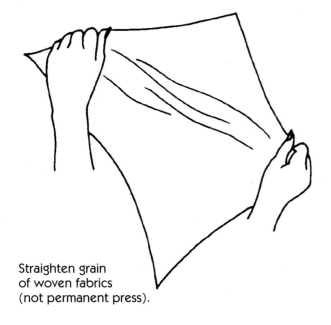

Straighten grain of woven fabrics (not permanent press).

GET READY, GET SET . . .
TO FUSE GARMENTS TOGETHER

Here's great news for all sewers and would-be sewers with time-crunched lives, or for those who want to try something new. You don't have to sew to make many of the clothes featured in this book. It may be hard to believe, but you can glue garments together in a couple of hours. Thanks to the interest in crafts, manufacturers have produced a variety of glues and fusible tapes that are washable, permanent, and invisible when dry. They're perfect for those of us who like to be creative with clothes.

If you want to try your hand at fusing garments, you'll need to use the right fabric and bonding product for your purposes. The fabric you select needs to have these characteristics:

◆ Tolerates ironing since you may be bonding seams together with fusible tape and an iron.

◆ Is thick enough so the glue line won't show through to outside of fashion fabric or be too stiff when dry.

◆ Has no nap and is not loosely woven or sheer.

◆ Is smooth or is woven with little texture.

◆ Is light- to medium-weight.

◆ Has a soft drape.

◆ Has a straight-grain.

SUGGESTED FABRICS FOR NO-SEW TECHNIQUES:

Cotton: Broadcloth, calico, cambric, challis, chambray, chintz, gingham, border prints (if wide enough to give desired length), permanent press, madras.

Silk: Jacquard, shantung, surah, noil.

Rayons: Challis, plain weave, linen-like.

Wool: Crepe, gabardine, light-weight flannel.

Synthetics: Cotton blend, such as polyester/cotton. If you use a plaid, make sure it's woven or printed with precision so the pattern will match at the side seams.

Knits: Double knits, interlocks, single knits, and sweatshirt knits without a pronounced one-way nap. Medium-weight, stable knits work best.

Get Your Fusible Tape and Glue

To use the no-sew method you'll need paper-backed fusible tape, and possibly fabric glue. There are many varieties to choose from, depending on the fabric and style you choose.

◆ HeatnBond® 3/8" (1cm) paper-backed fusible tape is what I used on all the projects photographed.

◆ Unique Stitch® fabric glue works well.

◆ Aleene's OK TO WASH-IT® is best for small, unstressed areas like hems.

◆ If you have a stretchy fabric like knits, try a glue made just for stretchable fabric, like Aleene's Flexible Stretchable®.

◆ Use a seam sealant like Fray Check® to seal the edges of ravelly fabric.

Be sure to choose a glue made for fabrics. It should be fast drying, washable, and permanent. Follow the instructions on the glue bottle. Some products are not dry-cleanable, so be sure to check on cleaning instructions. If you're in doubt, test it before you use it. Most companies have a customer hotline–800 phone number so you can ask questions.

For fusible tapes, be sure your iron is not hot or the bond won't hold. Follow the instructions on the fusing tape package.

Working With Fusible Tape

You can use fusible tape to construct garments two ways: clip-and-curve on neckline or armhole curves, and simple seam-fusing.

Clip-and-Curve Method

1 Cut 4"-5" (10-13cm) strips of fusible tape.

2 On one edge of tape make little snips every 1" (3cm), being careful not to cut all the way through the tape.

3 Fuse clipped tape strip onto the curve, 3/8" (1cm) in from the fabric edge.

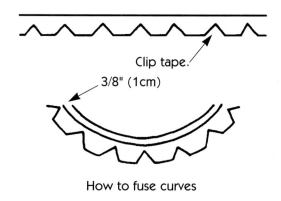

Clip tape.

3/8" (1cm)

How to fuse curves

4 Remove paper.

5 Fuse down the fabric edge. Make sure your iron is not hot.

Seam-Fusing Method

1 Fold and press a 3/8" (1cm) seam allowance to the wrong side on one of the edges that will be fused together.

2 Press 3/8" (1cm) fusing tape onto the seam allowance on the pressed side.

3 Peel off paper.

4 Position edge of the other side, right side down, over the exposed fusible tape.

5 Press to bond. Make sure your iron is not hot.

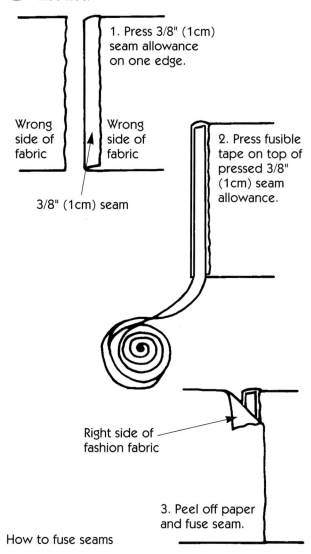

1. Press 3/8" (1cm) seam allowance on one edge.

Wrong side of fabric

Wrong side of fabric

3/8" (1cm) seam

2. Press fusible tape on top of pressed 3/8" (1cm) seam allowance.

Right side of fashion fabric

3. Peel off paper and fuse seam.

How to fuse seams

GET READY, GET SET . . .
FOR EASY WAYS TO MAKE CLOTHES FIT

An exciting feature of pattern-free fashions is that you shape them to fit *your* shape. In our own time, fashion innovator Issey Miyake demonstrates the striking results you get from taking a simple fabric shape and constructing it into a not-so-simple-looking garment. The fashions featured in this book are shaped by draping the fabric on your body and pinning tucks or pleats or gathers where you need them to create gentle shapes. The effect is soft, not tight, and shapes that flow gracefully and naturally with your body shape.

You can create decorative effects by shaping your fabric with tucks, pleats, belts, and gathers. After you've sewn, serged, or fused the basic pieces together, try the garment on in front of a mirror. Have your pins close at hand. Pinch the fabric to take tucks that shape the garment at the shoulder line, on the armhole, at the hem of the sleeve, at the hemline of a top, and at the waistline. Here are techniques to create the look you want.

Sleeve and Armhole Shaping

1 Make single or double tucks at the shoulder in armhole openings. Make sure the tucks are in the same position on both sides of the garment. Start by using 2" (5cm) of fabric in the tuck. Because the tuck is folded, the finished width on the outside of the garment is 1" (2.5cm), but you've taken 2" (5cm) of fullness out of your fabric.

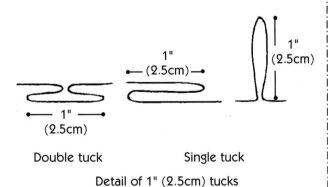

Double tuck   Single tuck

Detail of 1" (2.5cm) tucks

You can reduce the fullness even more by taking a 2-1/2" (6.5cm) or 3" (7.5cm) deep tuck. Fold the single tucks toward the garment front. This creates an interesting design detail, especially when you secure the tuck with a pretty button.

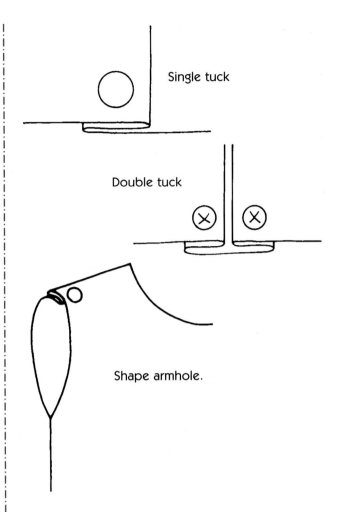

Single tuck

Double tuck

Shape armhole.

2 Make single or double tucks at the hem of the sleeve. Check to see that they are the same size and placed in the same position on each side. Start out with 1" (2.5cm) tucks and make them wider if you need to. Secure tucks with buttons or beads. For a more tailored look, make double tucks and stitch the folded edges together.

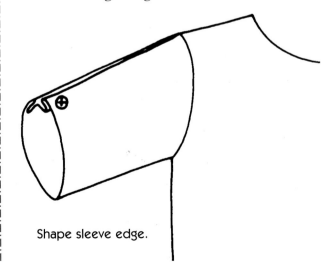

Shape sleeve edge.

3 To control the shape of the armhole, add a decorative trim band. You can sew or fuse this on.

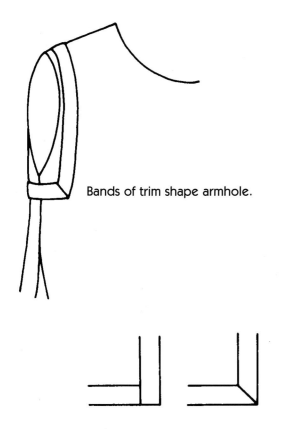

Bands of trim shape armhole.

For non-bias trim use square or mitered corners.

Bodice Shaping

1 Pinch a tuck, or pleat, vertically from the shoulder at least 7" (18cm) down toward the bust, and another 7" (18cm) down the back towards the waist. Make the tucks at least 3/4" (2cm) deep, and pull to bodice inside (sewing right side folds together) or create decorative detailing by leaving tuck on the outside (sewing wrong side folds together). If you want more shaping, make the tucks wide or create two long vertical tucks on each side.

After you stitch the tucks in place, you can topstitch, add decorative stitching, glue on trim, paint with fabric paint and stencils, or add buttons or whatever else appeals to you.

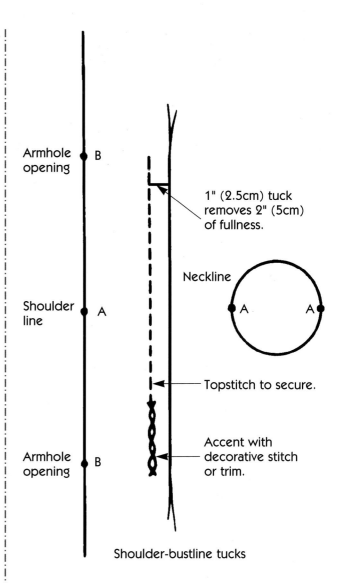

Armhole opening B

1" (2.5cm) tuck removes 2" (5cm) of fullness.

Neckline

Shoulder line A

A   A

Topstitch to secure.

Armhole opening B

Accent with decorative stitch or trim.

Shoulder-bustline tucks

2 Create hem tucks at the bottom hem of a top at least 3/4" (2cm) wide and however long you want. Start with two 7" (18cm) tucks aligned from the hem toward the bust, and adjust the length to suit your shape. You can make two hem tucks if you want to reduce the fullness.

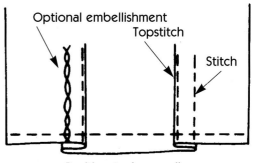

Optional embellishment
Topstitch
Stitch

Position tucks equally.

Tucks at hem shape hip and waist (like darts).

3 Add a belt, cut from the same or contrasting fabric, to shape a top, vest, or dress to your waist. You can easily fuse the belt pieces together and secure it to each side at the waist with some interesting button. You can make the belt in two sections and tie the ends in back, wrap them around the waist if it's a dress, or sew them together in back and decorate. (I add these belts as a great way to embellish the top with unusual details.)

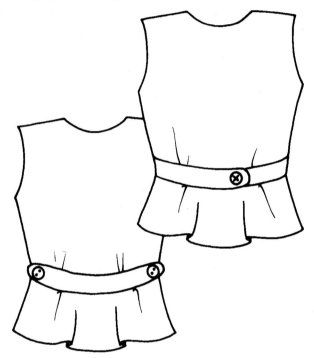

Belts in vest or bodice back

All-Purpose Shaping

1 Use elastic corded gathering tape to make gathers at the shoulders, below the bust, at the waist, or on sleeve hem.

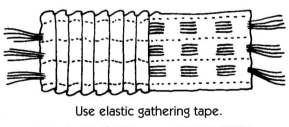

Use elastic gathering tape.

Make casing, insert soft elastic.

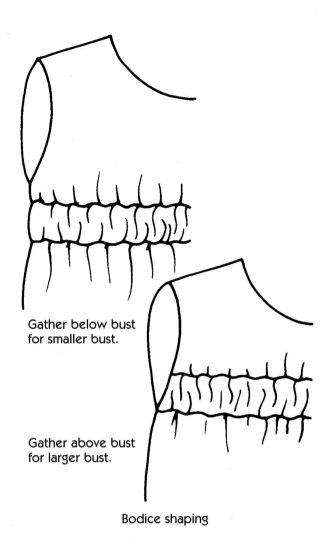

Gather below bust for smaller bust.

Gather above bust for larger bust.

Bodice shaping

2 For waist and sleeve hems make a casing, insert the elastic, and when suitable, topstitch.

GET READY, GET SET . . . TO HAVE FUN EMBELLISHING YOUR GARMENTS

The Exciting Possibilities of Decorative Trims

Those who enjoy creating with crafts know about the amazing array of decorative finishing trims available in a wide range of styles for all occasions. Those who are first-time sewers are in for a wonderful surprise. Most fabric stores carry a large assortment of trimmings in so many colors and designs that the difficulty lies in selecting the right one for your garment. The Resource List gives mail-order sources and other reliable companies to contact. For interesting ideas look at *Embellishments: Adding Glamour to Garments* by Linda Fry Kenzle (Chilton Book Company).

Here's a brief rundown of what's available to help you make successful choices:

◆ *Ready-made bias tapes* are available in cotton and rayon in many widths. They're useful for binding raw edges, or for making borders around neck openings, armholes, and hems.

◆ *Piping* is used as a decorative accent sewn into the seams of a garment.

◆ *Grosgrain ribbons* are used on lightweight fabrics to trim the edges of pointed collars, V-shaped necklines, pockets, and straight edges.

◆ *Rickrack* comes in many widths and is useful for curved edges.

◆ *Soutache* is a narrow braid identified by the middle "ditch" between two ridges. You can sew it on easily with just a single line of stitches down the center. It's available in cotton, rayon, and metallics.

◆ *Guimpe* is a shiny, thick braid with yarns twisted into a round pattern. Since it turns corners easily, use it for accenting curved lines.

◆ *Velvet ribbon, sequined braid,* and *pearl trim* are dramatic and beautiful trims for evening wear.

◆ *Leather* and *imitation suede braids* are heavy and best reserved for garments made in heavy fabrics, like jackets and coats.

◆ *Round cotton cord,* made in a range of colors and thicknesses, is great as a drawstring at the hemline of an over-blouse or jacket.

Guidelines for Selecting Trims

◆ Choose small, narrow trims for more form-fitting styles, and wider trims for large, loose-fitting garments.

◆ The weight of the trim needs to match the weight of the fabric. The garment will not hang properly if the weight of the trim is heavier than the fabric.

◆ For curvy design details, like necklines, select trim that will conform to the required curve either by stretching along the outer edge or by easing gently around the inner edge.

Guidelines for Attaching Trims

◆ Attach narrow trims 1/4" (6 mm) or narrower to fabric with one row of stitches, or one small line of glue, down the center of the trim. For wider trims, use a row of stitches, or a line of glue, along each edge.

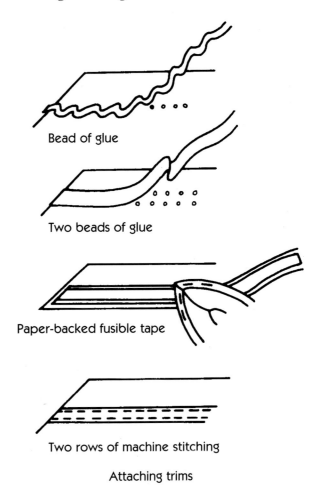

Bead of glue

Two beads of glue

Paper-backed fusible tape

Two rows of machine stitching

Attaching trims

◆ Choose the right glue for the job. There are special glues for stretchy fabrics, for gems and buttons, and for woven fabrics.

◆ To use bias tape along rounded edges, pre-shape the tape by pressing in a curve with a steam iron, then pin it in place and sew or glue.

Chic, Practical Topstitching, Decorative Machine Stitching, and Overlocking

Topstitching, decorative machine stitching, and overlock stitching with a serger are smart and practical ways to accent the lines of a garment. Not only do they create interesting design details on an otherwise boring garment, they often add stability to the garment.

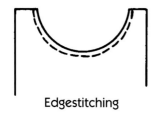

Edgestitching

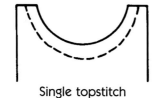

Single topstitch

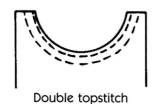

Double topstitch

Decorative machine stitching

Decorative machine stitching and topstitching

Topstitching with a sewing machine is a single row, or several parallel rows, of stitching on the right side of the fashion fabric at the seams or edges. It's very useful on lightweight fabrics because it helps maintain the shape along finished edges such as neck openings, facings, collars, and pockets. Edgestitching, a form of topstitching recommended in many of the following projects, is placed as close as possible to an edge or seam. Sergers create stunning overlock topstitching for edges and tucks.

Decorative machine stitching creates a beautiful finishing touch for many of these garments. In fact, the simplicity of these garments makes them perfect for any type of decorative stitching, from delicate to bold and dramatic. It is especially effective over the seams created by tucks. Any type of decorative stitching is highly visible so you need to do it carefully. For complete instructions, look at one of the books in the Resource List. Here are a few pointers for success:

◆ For topstitching and edgestitching, slightly loosen the upper tension on your sewing machine, and set the stitch length longer so topstitching will look uniform. Also use a walking foot on your machine if you have one.

◆ Some people find starching the fabric creates a smoother finish and prevents puckering for all types of decorative stitching.

◆ Use matching thread, or accentuate the decorative look by using a contrasting color or a thicker thread, especially when double topstitching, decorative machine stitching, or overlocking with your serger.

◆ You may want to draw your design on the fabric with fabric markers or chalk before embellishing.

◆ To keep topstitching or overlocking line straight, use the presser foot as a guide. Line up the edge of the foot to the fabric edge. You can also use narrow tape, the kind that quilters use, to mark the stitch line.

◆ For edgestitching or topstitching, if your machine has a needle adjustment for moving the needle, move it to the right. More of the presser foot will stay on the garment edge, helping the garment glide smoothly through the machine.

◆ When you come to the end of a stitched row, whether on your sewing machine or serger, knot the ends by hand on the inside if they'll show. To do this, leave several inches of the threads when you've finished stitching. Pull the top thread to the underside side of the garment, and tie a knot with the top and bobbin threads. Cut off the extra length.

GET READY, GET SET . . . GO!

This book is designed so that anyone can use it: beginning or experienced sewers. Some of the projects are great to do with children. Each chapter contains:

◆ Photographs of different looks you can create with the chapter project

◆ Creative ideas to get your imagination going

◆ Fabric recommendations and requirements

◆ Easy-to-use diagrams for making pattern shapes

◆ Step-by-step instructions, with references to this chapter, for serging, sewing, or fusing the garment together.

Since you'll need to refer back to this chapter, the edges of these pages stand out so you can easily flip back to them. If you need more help with serging, sewing, fusing, or fitting turn to the reference books listed in the Resource List at the end of the book.

Begin with any project you want to, and have fun creating fresh and imaginative fashions. I would love to hear about any of the pattern-free fashions you make, or any ideas you have for other designs. Write me at:

Open Chain Publishing
PO Box 2634-PFF
Menlo Park, CA
94026-2634

Left: Cotton print embellished with gold rickrack and gold buttons (Style #2)
Center: White satin acetate embellished with blue satin cording and pearl buttons (Style #3)
Right: Cotton knit embellished with serger threads (Style #1)

Chapter Two

Timeless Top

The 5000-year-old success story among clothing designs is a piece of cloth with a hole cut in the middle for your head. The Spanish word "poncho" is a familiar term for this easy-to-make, versatile garment. Variations of this timeless top are found all over the world. Most cultures have some version: fastened on the sides it becomes a Moroccan caftan or an African tunic; slit down the front, it changes into a Latin American ruana; add sleeves and a collar and it turns into a Chinese coat or a Japanese Happi coat.

One reason this classic garment has been around for thousands of years is that everyone can wear it. Cut it shorter or longer, wider or narrower—it looks good on men and women, young and old. Another reason for the popularity of this simple design is that it's so easy to make. As the following projects show, people with little time for sewing can put together a stunning garment in an hour. Beginning sewers find it easy to cut out and construct. In fact, it's so simple you can even iron it together with fusible fabric tape.

There are three models of the timeless top shown in this chapter, but if you glance through the rest of this book, you'll find other interpretations paired up with pants and skirt projects. The no-sew style is a perfect beginner project for a child or anyone who wants to get the feel of working with fabric.

PROJECTS

Style #1 featured here is a unisex serged sleeveless top, otherwise known as a tank top, which you can cut out and serge or sew in an hour. It fits a wide range of shapes for men or women. Make it smaller, and it will fit children. If you're a beginning sewer, this is a fail-safe project that gives you the chance to develop your serging or sewing skills while you complete a successful project. Try using different types of thread in your serger. If you're learning to use decorative stitches on your sewing machine, try one, two, or several around the neckline or hem or anywhere you want.

Style #2 is a simple top gently shaped with tucks at the shoulder and hem. Learn to sew or serge this top, and you'll use it over and over as a basic wardrobe piece. You can sew almost any type of fabric with this design to quickly create a blouse for any occasion. This is not a good design for fusing. Here it's shown in a casual cotton fabric with a playful design.

Style #3 requires no sewing. That's right, push your machine to the back of the table and glue this top together in record time. You can even wear it tonight. If you want to use your sewing machine or serger, please do so. But it's fun to try no-sew construction and learn about effective new materials borrowed from the craft and home-decorating fields. They provide time-conscious short cuts for making clothes for yourself or your family.

TIPS FOR PLANNING YOUR TOP

This simple design gives you the perfect chance to use fabric that has a bold color and pattern. All the fabrics mentioned for no-sew projects on page 6 are good for the tank top. Knit fabrics are a great choice, particularly if you have a serger and want to make a top quickly. If you choose to sew or serge this top, you can use a wider range of fabrics than what's on the list. Just make sure you don't use fabrics that are stiff or heavy, since they'll give the illusion you're heftier than you really are. Also avoid fabrics that fray easily.

WHAT TO BUY

◆ *Fabric:* The following yardage requirements for all three patterns in this chapter are for 45" (1.1m)–wide fabric. Buy the same amount for 54" (1.3m)–wide fabric. All hems and seam allowances are included. Refer to page 3 to determine your size.

Fabric Chart

	Child	Adult: 1	2	3	4
Short	1-1/8 yd (1m)	1-1/2 yd (1.4m)	1-1/2 yd (1.4m)	1-1/2 yd (1.4m)	1-2/3 yd (1.5m)
Long	1-1/3 yd (1.2m)	1-2/3 yd (1.5m)	1-3/4 yd (1.6m)	1-3/4 yd (1.6m)	1-3/4 yd (1.6m)

◆ *Patternmaking supplies:* Paper for making a pattern, pencils, eraser, straight edge or ruler, tailor's chalk or fabric marking pencils, measuring tape, scissors or rotary cutter and mat, and pins.

◆ *Decorative trim for neck, armhole openings, and hem:* 1 yd (91.5 cm) trim for neck, 40" (1m) for armholes, and double the width of the pattern measurements for the hem, if you want a decorative hem.

◆ *Matching or contrasting thread* for sewing or serging.

◆ *Fusible tape or fabric glue.* Check the instructions for gluing on page 6.

PREPARE YOUR FABRIC

Follow instructions on page 5 to wash and dry, or dryclean, your fabric prior to cutting.

CREATE TIMELESS TOP PATTERN AND CUT FABRIC

1 Choose the style you want to make.

2 Take your measurements to determine what size you need. If you're in doubt, refer to the section on shaping fabric to fit you on page 7.

• • • i d e a s • • •

◆ Create very different looks with rayon and dressier fabrics such as metallics, laces, or beaded and embroidered cloth. Fabrics with more dramatic texture or weave are also options as long as they drape softly and don't fray.

◆ Add different types of embellishment—fabric paints, button or bead designs, appliqués, or whatever inspires you—to create looks from casual to dressiest.

◆ If you have extra fabric, make a sash 3" (8cm) wide by 79" (2m) long, and wrap it around the blouse waist for a dramatic cummerbund.

◆ Make matching tops for children, or for a mother-and-daughter or father-and-son outfit.

◆ Use a beach towel or two to make a quick beach or pool coverup.

◆ Combine several coordinated fabrics across the width of the front and back, or place one fabric across the shoulders (points B front and back) and the second across the lower half of the top (from points B to points C front and back). You can use the same technique to create a couple of fun stripes.

◆ Make the tank top long, add side slits for ease of movement, and you have a dress.

◆ Coordinate your top with the Sure-Fit pants or shorts in Chapter Ten, the gathered skirt in Chapter Four, or sarong skirt in Chapter Twelve.

3 Refer to page 4 for creating your pattern shapes. Use the illustration Pattern Shapes for Timeless Top, Size 2, Short and Long.

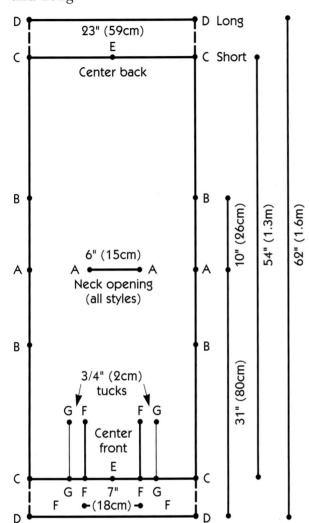

Pattern shapes for Timeless Top, size 2, short and long

Style #1, V-neck

Style #2, fusible neck

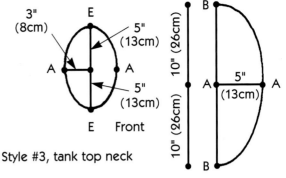

Style #3, tank top neck

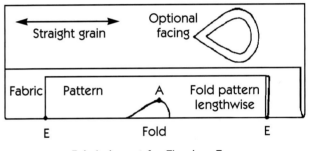

Style #3, tank top armholes

4 Pin the pattern shapes on the fabric as follows:

a. Fold fabric in half lengthwise.

b. Fold pattern pieces in half lengthwise (along points E).

c. Place center front and back (points E) along fold of fabric, using the fabric layout for placement of the rest of the pieces.

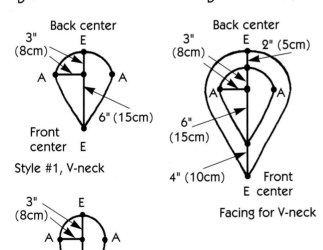

Fabric layout for Timeless Top

5 Cut the fabric using scissors or rotary cutter and mat.

6 Mark alphabet points with tailor's chalk or fabric markers.

CONSTRUCT YOUR TOP BY SEWING

1 Finish neck, armhole, and hem edges one of these ways:

◆ Zigzag raw edges, turn under 1/2" (1.3cm), press with an iron, and topstitch or hand hem. You can use a decorative machine stitch in a contrasting color thread to create a finished edge.

◆ Pin bias binding, or fabric or knit binding around openings and stitch in place. Topstitch if needed.

♦ Press edge under 1/4" (6mm). Stitch in place. Press it under another 1/2" (1.3cm), and finish by top-stitching, hand hemming, or blind hemming on your machine.

2 Create hem tucks between points F and G. Take 1" (2.5cm) tuck the length of F-F and G-G. Stitch and press towards side seams. Topstitch or decorative machine stitch along outside, pressed edge of tucks. You can also make the tuck on the inside of the fashion fabric and not topstitch.

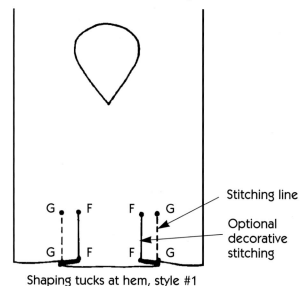

Shaping tucks at hem, style #1

3 Fold right sides together at points A, and pin side seams, matching points B and C. Sew seam and finish raw edges with zigzag or topstitching. You also can use French or flat-felled seams. Press seam.

4 Finish hemline with a decorative edging stitch, braid or trim, or by finishing raw edge, turning under, and topstitching or hemming.

5 To shape garment, pin tucks at armhole edge of shoulders, adjusting until the shape is pleasing. Press tucks in place and secure with decorative buttons or trim. See the section on shaping fabric to fit you on page 7 for more details.

CONSTRUCT YOUR TOP BY SERGING

1 Finish the neck and armhole edges first.

2 Fold right sides together at point A, and pin side seams from point B to point C. Serge the side seams between points B and C. Press flat to one side.

3 Serge the hem.

♦ If you want to add tucks, sew them as described above.

♦ Use four threads for a more dramatic look around the neck, arm, and hem edges. Try a contrasting thread color. If you are using a knit fabric, sew the side seams using three threads. Four threads make the seams stiffer and you need only three because knits don't ravel.

♦ If you want, stencil on a purchased design, or create your own with paints, stamps, appliqués, or whatever appeals to your unisex wearers. This is often easier to do on a flat piece of fabric, before you serge the side seams.

CONSTRUCT YOUR TOP BY FUSING

1 Place top wrong side up on your ironing board. Gently turn under neck edge 3/8" (1cm).

2 Use the clip-and-curve method outlined on page 7. Press under 3/8" (1cm) at neck edge of fashion fabric. Place clipped tape along fold of pressed edge, on wrong side of fashion fabric.

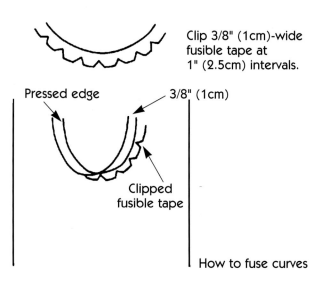

Clip 3/8" (1cm)-wide fusible tape at 1" (2.5cm) intervals.

Pressed edge

3/8" (1cm)

Clipped fusible tape

How to fuse curves

Allow tape to cool before peeling off paper backing. If you need to, pin the turned edge in place right on top of the fusible tape, pushing the pins into the ironing board. Press in place, being sure not to overheat.

3 Press the entire length of both side seam edges under 3/8" (1cm).

4 To create armhole opening, place 3/8" (1cm) wide fusible tape on wrong side of fabric, *under* the turned seam allowance from point B to point B (B-A-B). Press tape. After tape cools, peel off backing. Press the seam allowance onto the fusible surface. The armhole is finished. Repeat for other side of top.

5 To create side seams, on bodice back place 3/8" (1cm) fusible tape on *top* of turned seam allowance between points B and C. Press tape.

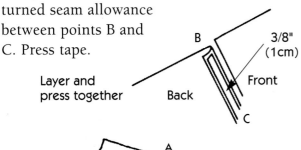

Layer and press together

Back

Front

B

C

3/8" (1cm)

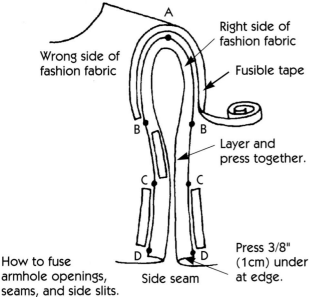

Wrong side of fashion fabric

Right side of fashion fabric

Fusible tape

Layer and press together.

Press 3/8" (1cm) under at edge.

A

B B

C C

D D

Side seam

How to fuse armhole openings, seams, and side slits.

After tape cools, peel off backing. Place the pressed under seam allowance of the bodice front on top of bodice back seam allowance, matching B-C on both sides. Press to fuse seams together. Repeat for other side of top. Clip front seam allowance above and below fusible tape, if necessary.

6 Finish the side slits between points C and D like the armhole openings. Place 3/8" (1cm) wide fusible tape on wrong side of fabric, *under* the turned seam allowance from point C to point D. Press tape. After tape cools, peel off backing. Press the seam allowance onto the fusible surface. Half the side slit is finished. Repeat for other side of slit and then repeat for other side of top.

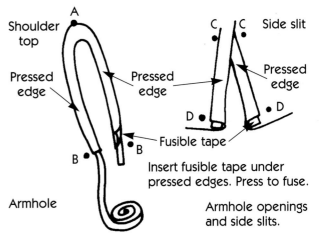

Shoulder top

A

C C Side slit

Pressed edge

Pressed edge

Pressed edge

D D

B B

Fusible tape

Armhole

Insert fusible tape under pressed edges. Press to fuse.

Armhole openings and side slits.

7 Turn raw edge of hem under 1/4" (6mm) and press. Turn and press 1" (2.5 cm) hem. Fuse in place with tape.

8 Cut trim to fit neckline and glue in place using fabric glue. Make sure all raw edges are tucked under.

9 To shape garment, pin tucks at shoulder, adjusting until the shape is pleasing. Press tucks in place. Secure with fusing tape, or glue down trim or braid over tucks to hold them in place. You can also sew on buttons. For further instructions, turn to the section on shaping fabric to fit you on page 7.

FINISHING TOUCHES

You can glue matching trim around armholes, and create whatever designs you want with the smooth surface of your top. Create with buttons, paints, glitter, beads, or whatever suits your fancy.

Enjoy wearing these tops, either tucked in or as an overblouse, with coordinated pants or a skirt for a stunning outfit. Or make the man or boys in your life tank tops they'll love to wear.

Left: Polyester bodice, sleeves, and coordinated facing with decorative buttons (Style #1 variation without shoulder tucks)
Center: Linen embellished with coconut shell buttons (Style #1)
Right: Brushed fleece with satin cording drawstring and cotton/synthetic blend ribbing at cuffs and collar (Style #2)

Classic Blouse & Turtleneck Top

The simplest top, featured in Chapter Two, is reborn in these projects to become an elegant blouse and a turtleneck top.

PROJECTS

Style #1, a crisp linen blouse, and Style #2, a man's or woman's turtleneck top, suggest the variety of wardrobe needs you can meet with this top. It can be sized for children or adults, men or women, large sizes or petites. It can change to suit your seasonal needs—make it as an airy eyelet blouse for summer or a cozy Polartec pullover for winter. The variations in this chapter include two sleeve lengths; the short sleeve goes to the elbow, and the long sleeve goes to the wrist.

TIPS FOR PLANNING YOUR CLASSIC BLOUSE OR TURTLENECK TOP

You'll need to sew or serge the turtleneck top, but you can fuse, serge, or sew the classic blouse. Don't use fabric that has a nap or print going in only one direction.

◆ If you sew the top together, you can use any light- to medium-weight fabric of your choice.

◆ If you serge the top together, you can use a 4-thread stitch with contrasting color threads to finish the neck, sleeve, and hem edges. Use 3 threads to serge seams if you're using a knit fabric. If you have a woven fabric that could fray, use the 4-thread stitch.

◆ If you fuse the top together, use one of the fabrics listed on page 6. Remember that the fused seams and edges will be stiffer.

WHAT TO BUY

◆ *Fabric:* All hems and seam allowances are included in the fabric requirements given below which are calculated for 45" (1.1m)-wide fabric. Purchase extra fabric if you need to match a stripe or pattern.

Fabric Chart

	Child	Adult: 1	2	3	4
Short Sleeve	1-1/4 yd (1m)	1-2/3 yd (1.5m)	1-2/3 yd (1.5m)	1-2/3 yd (1.5m)	1-2/3 yd (1.5m)
Long Sleeve	1-1/4 yd (1.1m)	2-1/3 yd (2.2m)	2-1/3 yd (2.2m)	2-1/3 yd (2.2m)	2-1/3 yd (2.2m)

◆ *Patternmaking supplies:* Paper such as tissue or butcher paper, or pattern paper, pencils and eraser, straight edge or ruler, tailor's chalk or fabric marking pencils, measuring tape, scissors and pins.

◆ *Decorative braids, ribbons, appliqués, buttons, or paints* if you choose to embellish the blouse.

◆ *Thread* to match fabric, or contrast, if you use a decorative stitch.

◆ *1/2 yd (46cm) ribbed knit* for collar, cuffs, and optional ribbed hem.

PREPARE YOUR FABRIC

Follow instructions on page 5 to wash and dry, or dryclean, your fabric prior to cutting.

CREATE BLOUSE OR TURTLENECK PATTERN AND CUT FABRIC

1 Choose the style you want to make.

2 Take your measurements to determine what size you need. If you're in doubt, refer to the section shaping fabric to fit you on page 7.

3 Choose the shape you want for the neckline. Check out the necklines and instructions on page 5 for more variations. You can alter the blouse pattern, shaping the neck opening so it's the most flattering for you. If you're fusing this together, choose a round neckline. Whatever your choice of neckline, you need to decide on how you want to finish it, with a facing out of the same or contrasting fabric, with purchased binding, or with decorative trim.

4 Refer to the instructions in the section on patterns made of squares and rectangles on page 4 to create your pattern. Use the pattern shapes for the Classic Top, Style #1, Size 2, and for the Turtleneck, Style #2, Size 2.

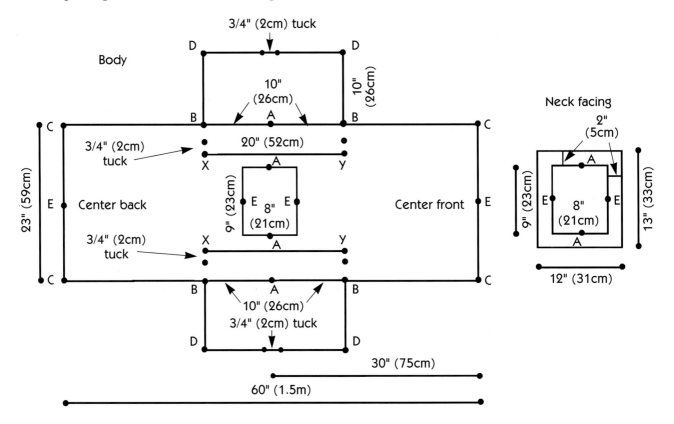

Pattern shapes for classic top, short sleeves, style #1, size 2

✦ ✦ ✦ i d e a s ✦ ✦ ✦

- ◆ Try an overblouse with a drawstring at the bottom.
- ◆ To make a great sweatshirt for a child, use sweatshirt fleece and finish neck, sleeve, and bottom edges with narrow knit ribbing.
- ◆ This style is perfect for special fabrics, like handwoven yardage or Raschel knits. Don't try any fabric that frays or doesn't have a soft drape.

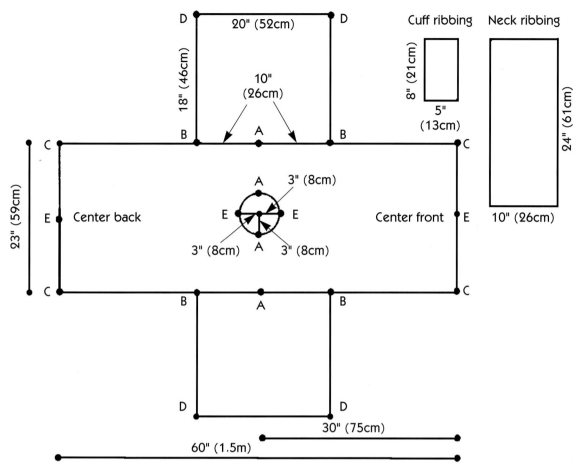

Pattern shapes for turtleneck, style #2, size 2.

5 Pin the pattern shapes on the fabric as follows:

a. Fold fabric in half lengthwise.

b. Fold pattern pieces in half lengthwise (along points E).

c. Place center front and back (points E) along fold of fabric using layouts in Fabric Layout for Blouse and Fabric Layout for Turtleneck. Place sleeve pattern on selvage side of fabric, and do not fold pattern.

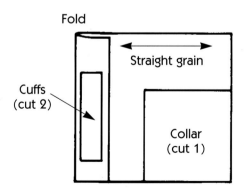

Fabric layout for ribbed knit for turtleneck

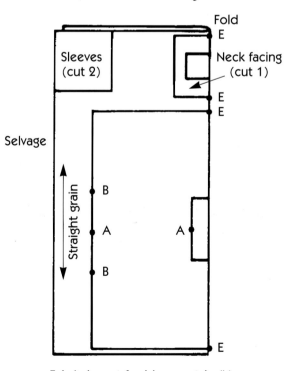

Fabric layout for blouse, style #1

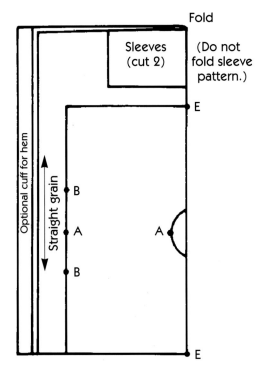

Fabric layout for turtleneck, style #2

6 Cut the fabric using scissors or rotary cutter and mat.

7 Mark alphabet points with tailor's chalk or fabric markers.

8 For simplest construction, cut the sleeves straight then shape with tucks and decorate with buttons. However, you can also experiment with a slightly tapered sleeve or a rolled back cuff.

CONSTRUCT YOUR CLASSIC BLOUSE

Finish Neckline

You may choose to fuse, serge, or sew the blouse together.

Sew or Serge:

1 Staystitch neckline edge to prevent stretching.

2 Attach interfacing, unless fabric has enough body to lie flat without it, to neckline facing or collar (fuse with iron, or baste with machine).

3 Finish edges of facing. Right sides together, sew facing to neckline edge with a 1/2" (1.3 cm) seam allowance. Trim.

Press facing under. If you want, topstitch around neck edge. (Optional: Stitch in ditch for more polished look.)

Tips for Serging:

◆ Use four threads for a more decorative look.

◆ If you have thin materials like georgette crepe, crepe de chine, silk, lightweight cottons, rayons, or synthetics, try a rolled hem or a shell hem.

◆ For thicker fabrics use decorative threads like embroidery floss or wooly nylon to create a more substantial look that matches the fabric.

Fuse:

1 Trim raw neck edge so it's smooth; then turn under 3/8" (1cm) and press.

2 Cut strip and clip curves in paper-backed 3/8" (1cm) wide fusible tape.

3 For further fusing instructions, turn to page 6. Be sure iron is not too hot.

Attach Sleeves

1 Place sleeves and bodice right sides together matching point A on sleeve with point A on shoulder top.

2 Pin and sew or serge sleeve in place. For fusing instructions, turn to page 6.

3 Press seam toward sleeve.

4 Topstitch if you desire.

Sew Side Seams

1 Right sides together, serge, sew, or fuse entire side seam, from sleeve ends, point D, to hem, point C, matching underarms at point B. For details on how to fuse seams, see page 6.

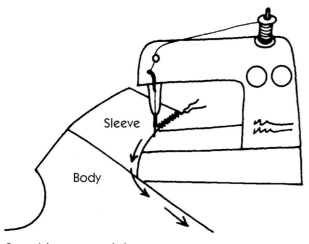

Sleeve

Body

Sew side seam and sleeve.

2 Press seams open or to one side if you're topstitching.

Finish Hems

1 To finish sleeve and bodice hems, press under raw edges 1/4" (6mm), then turn and press at least a 1" (2.5cm) hem allowance. Fuse or hem with your machine or by hand. You can also make a serged finish on the hem edge.

2 For a more fitted sleeve, take one or two tucks at finished sleeve bottom. Hold in place with decorative buttons.

Embellish

Finish sleeve, neckline, and hemline (if this is to be an overblouse) with braid, trim, decorative machine stitching, overlocking, or other embellishment. For more details, turn to the sections on shaping fabric to fit you on page 7 and embellishing your garments on page 10.

CONSTRUCT YOUR TURTLENECK

Follow instructions for the blouse with these differences:

◆ Use knit or some type of stretch fabric.

◆ Use pattern shapes for turtleneck (high round neck and long sleeves).

◆ Do not fuse or glue. Serging is best. If you use your sewing machine, adjust the stitch for knits and use a ball point needle.

◆ Use the bottom cuff as a casing to add a drawstring tie. It will create a decorative finishing touch, and on a cold day you can adjust it for a snug, warmer fit.

FINISHING TOUCHES

The blouse style looks great under a suit, over pants, or as an evening blouse in silk combined with a soft skirt. Try the turtleneck with leggings or stirrup pants. Because of the easy fit, delight a friend or family member with a warm, fleecy Polartec turtleneck.

Create an outfit by coordinating a classic blouse or turtleneck top with the Sure-Fit pants or shorts in Chapter Ten, the gathered skirt in Chapter Four, or the sarong skirt in Chapter Twelve.

Left: Raw silk skirt (Style #2)
    accented with coconut shell button,
    and a linen blouse
Right: Crinkle cotton skirt (Style #1)
    with purchased blouse

Gathered Skirt

Thanks to an innovative sewing product, there's an easy way to gather the waistband on a skirt. The product is an elastic gathering tape such as Stitch & Stretch®. To use it, you sew the flat tape onto your flat fashion fabric, pull the gathering cords, and *presto!*, you have a gathered skirt with a pretty waistband. Of course you can always make the traditional elastic waistband with a casing, also featured in this chapter. Make it with waistband elastic guaranteed not to roll (it really doesn't) or insert regular elastic, which is soft and less bulky so that you can topstitch it in place.

Tips For Planning Your Skirt

This design requires a sewing machine. You can also make it with a serger and sewing machine, or with fusing tape and a sewing machine. It is suitable for a wide variety of fabrics that gracefully gather, so you can create anything from a toddler's knit skirt to a dressy evening statement. Test the fabric by folding it into your hand. Does it fall into soft folds or is it stiff? Is it going to lie flat or give you a bulky waistline? Good choices are lightweight knits, a wide range of cottons or cotton/synthetics, rayon, silk, lightweight flannel, fine corduroy and wool blends.

Projects

Style #1, the broomstick skirt, takes an hour to make. It features the widest Stitch & Stretch gathering band at the waist, several yards of cotton crinkle cloth, and only one seam. After you finish sewing, wet the skirt, twist it tight to wring out the water, and either tie the twisted skirt into a knot, or put it in a lingerie bag and dry it in the drier.

The straight skirt, Style #2, is silk pongee with a simple casing at the waistband and topstitched elastic. It too has only one seam with a fake fly front and button closure.

What to Buy

◆ *Fabric:* All the following yardage requirements are for fabric that is 45" (1.1m) wide. The finished length of the child's skirt is 18" (45.5cm). The finished length of both adult skirts is 34" (87cm). All measurements for the gathered skirt variations include hems, seam allowances, and elastic casing.

Fabric Chart

	Child	Adult	
		Size: 1/2	3/4
Full	1-1/3 yd (1.3m)	2 yd (1.9m)	2 yd (1.9m)
Straight	2/3 yd (60cm)	1 yd (.95m)	2 yd (1.9m)

◆ *Patternmaking supplies:* Paper for making a pattern, pencils and eraser, straight edge or ruler, tailor's chalk or fabric marking pencils, measuring tape, scissors and pins. Experienced sewers can choose to cut out this skirt without making a paper pattern.

◆ *Non-roll waistband elastic, regular elastic, or elastic gathering tape.* You can get elastic gathering tape at fabric stores or through mail-order catalogs. Please refer to the Resource List at the end of this book for suggestions on where to buy tape. A widely available brand is Stitch & Stretch® which comes in 1", 1-1/2" and 2-1/4" widths. If you're unsure of which to choose, do a test with all three types of elastic and then figure out your design.

◆ *Matching thread* for sewing or serging. If you want to create a smocking effect, or use decorative stitching as a design element, choose one or more contrasting thread colors.

◆ If you want to fuse or glue the seams together, buy *fusible tape* or *fabric glue*.

PREPARE YOUR FABRIC

Follow instructions on page 5 to wash and dry, or dryclean, your fabric prior to cutting.

CREATE GATHERED SKIRT PATTERN SHAPES AND CUT FABRIC

1 Choose the style you want to make.

2 Take your measurements to determine what size you need. If you're in doubt, refer to the section on shaping fabric to fit you on page 4.

3 To create your pattern shapes, refer to the instructions on page 4, and the illustration Pattern Shapes and Layouts for Gathered Skirt. The pattern includes allowance for sewing on gathering tape. If you want to make a casing and use regular waistband elastic instead of the gathering tape, add the width of your elastic plus 3/4" (2cm) across the top of the skirt pattern.

◆ ◆ ◆ i d e a s ◆ ◆ ◆

◆ Make a dropped waist skirt. Create a top panel with a little fullness and a bottom panel with as much fullness as desired. Use a narrow elastic gathering tape to gather the bottom into the top panel, and a wide elastic gathering tape to give a smocking effect at the waist.

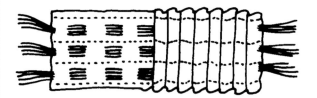

Elastic corded gathering tape

◆ Make a three-tiered skirt. Use the same technique as the dropped waist skirt and add fullness to each panel as shown in the illustration. Buy 2-1/2 yd (2.3m) of 45" (1.1m)-wide fabric, 1-1/8 yd (1m) wide elastic gathering tape, and 6-1/2 yd (6m) narrow elastic gathering tape. See the Tiered Skirt Design for cutting the fabric.

◆ Showcase special fabrics like prepleated and crinkle cottons.

◆ For an elegant evening skirt use chiffon or soft lace with a liner made separately. Use the same pattern for the liner, but make it without so much fullness and use narrow elastic gathering tape at the waistband.

◆ Try the slim skirt with the slit at the back or the side, or make it a short skirt.

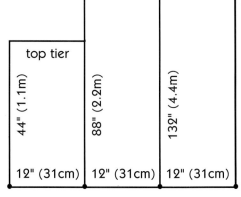

Tiered skirt design

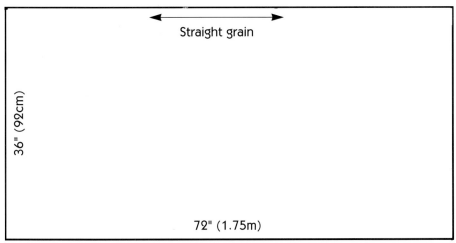

Straight grain

36" (92cm)

72" (1.75m)

Style #1, Size 1/2

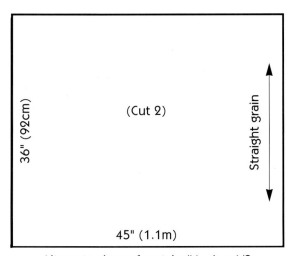

36" (92cm)

(Cut 2)

Straight grain

45" (1.1m)

Alternate shape for style #1, size 1/2

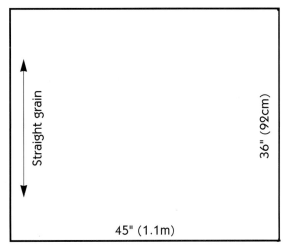

Straight grain

36" (92cm)

45" (1.1m)

Style #2, size 1/2

Pattern shapes and layout for gathered skirt

4 Use the fabric layout in the illustration Pattern Shapes and Layout for Gathered Skirt. Pin the pattern shapes on the fabric as follows:

a. Fold fabric in half lengthwise.

b. Fold pattern pieces in half lengthwise (along points E).

c. Place center front and back (points E) along fold of fabric.

5 Cut the fabric using scissors or rotary cutter and mat.

6 Mark alphabet points with tailor's chalk or fabric markers.

CONSTRUCT YOUR SIMPLE GATHERED SKIRT

1 Turn and press 1/2" (1.3 cm) of the top (waistline) edge of the fashion fabric to the inside.

2 Cut the gathering tape the same length as the top edge of the fabric.

3 Sew gathering tape 1/4" (6mm) from top fold on wrong side of fabric, stitching along all the lines printed on the tape.

4 Gather the elastic cords on the tape until it fits your waist.

5 Adjust gathers so the fullness is even around the skirt, then sew the elastic cords in place at each end of the tape. Use a satin stitch or sew several times with a straight stitch to reinforce. If the elastic cording releases, you will no longer have a gathered skirt!

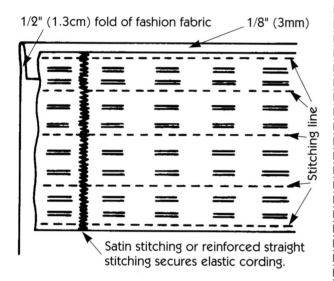

1/2" (1.3cm) fold of fashion fabric   1/8" (3mm)

Stitching line

Satin stitching or reinforced straight stitching secures elastic cording.

How to use elastic gathering tape.

6 Cut the extra cording.

7 Pin the side seam, right sides together, from the waist to the hem.

8 Sew the seam with your serger, or use your sewing machine to stitch and finish the seam.

9 If needed, trim hem so it hangs evenly.

10 Press hem edge under 1/4" (6mm), or if you have a serger, serge hem edge. Turn finished edge of hem under another 2" (5cm), press and sew or hand-hem in place. If you are using sheer fabric you may want to make a rolled hem.

CONSTRUCT YOUR SIMPLE STRAIGHT SKIRT

1 Sew, serge, or fuse seams together (following instructions for fusing on page 6) leaving a slit at the bottom for walking ease if you need it. With your sewing machine, stitch a 1" (2.5cm) single tuck down the entire center front, from the waist to the slit, if you want to create a fake fly front.

2 At waistband, press under raw edge 1/4" (6mm) or finish with serger.

3 Make casing. Turn under the width of your waistband elastic plus 1/2" (1.3cm). Press and sew as close to the edge of the casing as you can, leaving a 3" (7.5cm) opening to thread the elastic through the casing.

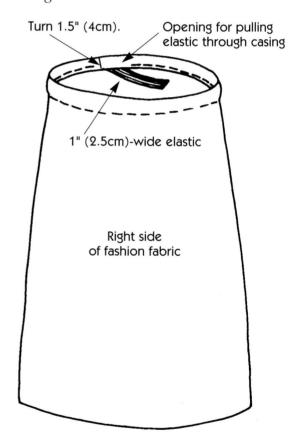

Turn 1.5" (4cm).

Opening for pulling elastic through casing

1" (2.5cm)-wide elastic

Right side of fashion fabric

Waistband casing for style #2

4 Cut waistband elastic slightly less than your waistline measurement plus 1/2" (1.3cm) for lapping. Usually, the narrower the elastic, the shorter it will have to be.

5 Pull elastic through casing, lap the two ends together, stitch securely, and sew up the casing opening.

6 If using regular elastic, topstitch one or more rows to secure the elastic in the casing and to give a flattering finish to the waist.

FINISHING TOUCHES

Those who can't live without pockets can make a pattern from their favorite patch pocket and add pockets to one or both sides of the skirt front. Measure and place them where they're convenient for you. Add interesting buttons down the center front of either style. Have fun wearing your skirt with different blouses and t-shirts. If you make one of the simple tops featured in this book of out of the same fabric, you'll have a two-piece dress.

*Left: Cotton chambray embellished with
stencilling and pearl buttons (Style #2)
Right: Bodice of cotton batiste, skirt of cotton
novelty print; rickrack, buttons, and fused
appliqué embellishment (Style #1)*

Chapter Five

Simplest Dress & Jumper

The simplest way to make a dress or jumper is to sew or serge a skirt onto a suitable top. That's exactly what the projects in this chapter show you how to do. If you want a sleeveless dress or jumper, add the skirt to the sleeveless Timeless Top in Chapter Two. If you want a dress with sleeves to the elbow or wrist, add the skirt to the blouse with sleeves in Chapter Three.

PROJECTS

Style #1 shows a child's high-waist dress, and Style #2, a woman's drop-waist dress. The skirts are easy to make. If you don't know how to run a simple gathering stitch on your sewing machine, purchase elastic gathering tape, introduced in Chapter Four, to fit the skirt to the top. You can satisfy your creative impulses by trying the many different gathering tapes available—the wider tapes suggest a smocking effect. Don't forget to look in the home decoration section of your fabric store or mail-order catalog for interesting curtain gathering tapes. Get ready to have fun with these projects, and best of all, have an attractive dress to wear in an afternoon or evening.

TIPS FOR PLANNING YOUR DRESS OR JUMPER

Both of the projects in this chapter require sewing. You can serge or fuse many of the seams, but you will need your sewing machine to sew on the gathering tape.

For fabric suggestions, please turn to the section on fabrics on page 6. Remember that a fuller skirt should be made with lighter weight, drapey fabric.

WHAT TO BUY

◆ *Fabric:* The following fabric requirements for 45" (1.1m) wide fabric assume a mid-calf length, but of course you can alter the pattern to have the hemline anywhere you want, from your ankle to your thigh.

Fabric Chart

	Child	Adult: 1	2	3	4
Empire Waist					
Style #1	2-1/2 yds (2.3m)	3 yds (2.75m)	3 yds (2.75m)	3 yds (2.75m)	3-1/4 yds (3m)
Dropped Waist					
Style #2	2 yds (1.85m)	2-2/3 yds (2.5m)	2-2/3 yds (2.5m)	2-2/3 yds (2.5m)	2-2/3 yds (2.5m)

◆ *Patternmaking supplies:* Paper for making a pattern, pencils and eraser, straight edge or ruler, tailor's chalk or fabric marking pencils, measuring tape, scissors, and pins.

◆ *1/2 yd (46cm) light- or medium-weight (depending on your fabric) fusible interfacing* for neck opening.

◆ *Elastic gathering tape* which you'll find at your fabric store or through one of the mail-order suppliers in the Resource List. A widely available product is Stitch & Stretch®. Buy the same length as the yardage you're using for your skirt.

◆ *Thread* to match the fabric or contrast with it if you use a decorative stitch.

◆ *Decorative braids, ribbons, appliqués, paints, or other embellishments.*

◆ *Buttons* to finish the shoulder shaping tucks, if you are using them.

PREPARE YOUR FABRIC

Follow instructions on page 5 to wash and dry, or dryclean, your fabric prior to cutting.

CREATE DRESS/JUMPER PATTERN SHAPES AND CUT FABRIC

1 Choose the style you want to make.

2 Take your measurements to determine what size you need. If you're in doubt, refer to the section on shaping fabric to fit you on page 7.

3 Choose the shape you want for the neckline. Check out the necklines and instructions on page 5 for more variations. You can alter the pattern for the dress or bodice to whatever neck opening is the most flattering for you.

4 To create your pattern shapes, refer to the instructions in the section on patterns made of squares and rectangles on page 4, and the illustrations Pattern Shapes for High-Waisted Child's Dress/Jumper and Pattern Shapes for Women's Drop-Waist Dress, Style #2, Size 2.

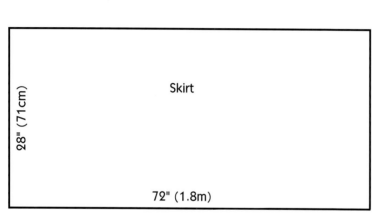

Pattern shapes for high-waisted child's dress/jumper, style #1

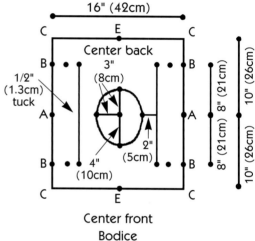

ideas

◆ Create different looks by changing the lengths of the bodice and skirt:

Empire

Cut the bodice length under the armhole opening. If you're large busted, the gathered skirt should be attached above your bustline. If you're small busted, the skirt can come below your bustline, but above your waist. This style doubles as a great maternity dress. It's also a popular style for girls. The girl's dress featured has a modified empire waist.

Easy waist

Cut the bodice length so the skirt will start at your waistline. Add a belt or make a sash out of leftover fabric. A versatile sash measurement is 4" (10cm) by 2 yd (1.8m). Either sew a rolled or turned hem all the way around the sash, or fold it in half lengthwise, press the edges under 1/4" (6mm) and edgestitch in place. You can also wear this style loose, without a belt or sash, and use it as a jumper to wear over T-shirts or blouses.

◆ Add sleeves, using the Classic Blouse or Turtleneck patterns in Chapter Three.

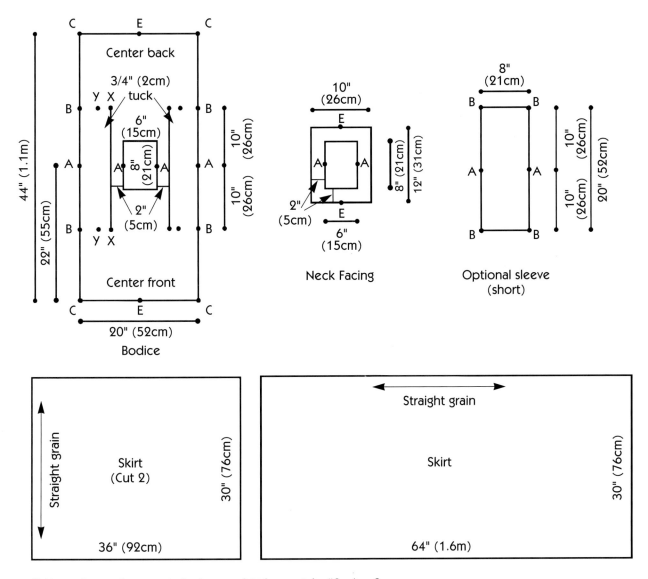

Pattern shapes for women's drop-waist dress, style #2, size 2

5 Use the fabric layouts in the illustrations that follow.

For Style #1, Child's High-Waist Dress/Jumper:

a. Fold fabric in half lengthwise.

b. Fold pattern pieces in half lengthwise (along points E).

c. Place center front and back (points E) along fold of fabric.

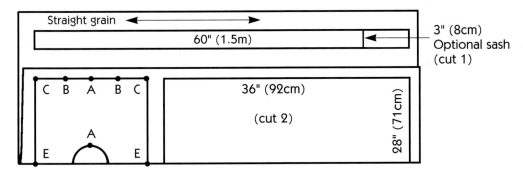

Fabric layout for child's dress, style #1   Woven fabrics with non-directional pattern

For Style #2, Adult Drop-Waist Dress/Jumper:

a. Fold fabric in half lengthwise.

b. Fold bodice pattern in half across the width or lengthwise (along points E).

c. Place bodice fold on fabric fold.

d. Fold other pattern pieces in half lengthwise (along points E). Place center front and back (points E) along fold of fabric.

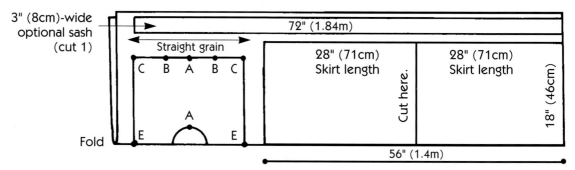

3" (8cm)-wide optional sash (cut 1)

72" (1.84m)

Straight grain

C B A B C

A

28" (71cm) Skirt length

28" (71cm) Skirt length

Cut here.

18" (46cm)

Fold

E   E

56" (1.4m)

Fabric layout for child's dress, style #1

For knits and wovens with vertical patterns

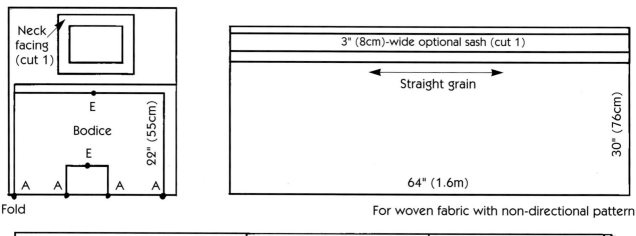

Neck facing (cut 1)

E

Bodice

E

22" (55cm)

A   A   A   A

Fold

3" (8cm)-wide optional sash (cut 1)

Straight grain

30" (76cm)

64" (1.6m)

For woven fabric with non-directional pattern

Neck facing (cut 1)

Bodice

B A B

A

E   E

Straight grain

Cut here.

Skirt length 30" (76cm)

Skirt length 30" (76cm)

18" (46cm)

Fold

Fabric layout for woman's dress, style #2

For knits and wovens with vertical patterns

6 Cut the fabric using scissors or rotary cutter and mat.

NOTE:

◆ Whatever your choice of neckline, unless you're serging or finishing the neck edges with binding or decorative trim, you'll need to make a facing with matching interfacing, After you cut neck facing from fashion fabric, use same pattern to cut interfacing.

◆ When you cut skirt lengths, note the layout for cutting two skirt panels. Use this if your fabric is a knit or woven with a vertical pattern that needs to have the straight grain running from waist to hem and therefore isn't wide enough to make a skirt. You'll need to sew the two panels together.

◆ Cut optional sash out of remaining fabric.

7 Mark alphabet points with tailor's chalk or fabric markers.

CONSTRUCT YOUR DRESS/JUMPER

Bodice

The top of the dress is based on the Timeless Top pattern in Chapter Two. Please turn to the step-by-step instructions in Chapter Two for constructing this top by serging, sewing, or fusing, but don't make a hem. Follow the illustration for shaping the bodice on page 9.

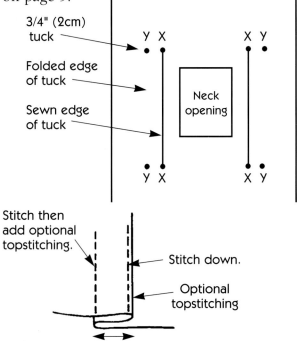

Bodice shaping

Skirt

You may sew the skirt or use a combination of sewing and serging, or sewing and fusing.

1 If you know how to create gathers with your sewing machine, sew, serge, or fuse the skirt seams together then gather at the waist to fit the bodice.

2 If you are using gathering tape, you need an open seam. If you have only one skirt seam, leave it open. If you have two seams, sew or serge one of them together and press.

3 Sew gathering tape on wrong side of top edge of skirt. Follow instructions on gathering tape package for this step.

4 Gather the elastic cords on the tape until skirt gathers to fit bodice bottom edge.

5 Securely topstitch or zigzag ends of gathering tape to hold elastic cords in place, and trim off the extra ends.

6 Sew or serge remaining side seam of skirt.

7 Right sides together, pin gathered skirt onto bodice. Adjust gathers so side seams match bodice side seams.

8 Sew, making sure gathers lie flat and even. Press seam toward bodice. Topstitch on outside for a smoother look.

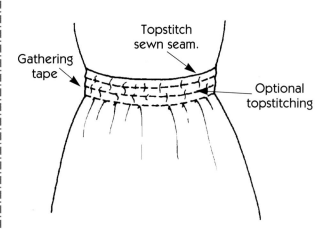

Topstitch bodice/skirt seam.

Hems

1 Finish armhole edges according to instructions for Timeless Top on page 19.

2 Turn skirt hem under 1/4" (6mm), press, and turn under again 1-1/2" (4cm). Use your machine to blind hem or topstitch in place, or hand-hem.

FINISHING TOUCHES

Add whatever decorative trims, braids, or buttons you want. Decorative machine stitching looks great at the bottom of the bodice and hem. Pair the sleeveless dress with a blouse or fitted knit top for an outfit you'll feel comfortable wearing all day—to work, to shop, to cook dinner, or to go out to dinner.

*Left (Style #1) and Right (Style #2):
Cotton/synthetic blend with satin
ribbon, eyelet, and lace accents*

Swirling Gown

Would you like a swirling new night-gown that is both comfortable and lovely? Pair a flattering, soft fabric with a simple, flowing shape, and you can make up a gorgeous nightgown in a few hours.

PROJECTS

The utterly feminine gowns shown as Style #1 and Style #2 belie their simple construction. They look complicated but are really modifications of the simple tops in Chapter Two and Chapter Three. What is added is elastic gathering tape that gathers the shoulder to whatever width you desire. Finish with lace edging or eyelet inserts and bows. It's as easy as that.

TIPS FOR PLANNING YOUR SWIRLING GOWN

You'll need to sew the gathering tape onto the shoulder line, but you can sew or serge the rest of this garment. I don't recommend fusing because it stiffens the fabric and makes it uncomfortable for sleeping.

For a summer version, choose lightweight fabrics that are soft and gentle next to your skin. Nylon tricot, cotton (woven or knits), and cotton/synthetic blends are good choices. Keep in mind that the gathering tape will show through sheer fabrics. If you want to use lace or chiffon, you'll need to line the gown. Treat the sheer fabric and lining as one unit.

WHAT TO BUY

◆ *Fabric:* The following fabric require-ments for sleeveless and long sleeve gown styles use 45" (1.1m)-wide fabric.

The hem length for the gown is 40" (1m), which is below the knee, but you can change the hem or sleeve to any length. Just change the amount of fabric you buy.

Fabric Chart

	Child	Adult	
		Size: 1/2	3/4
Gown	1-2/3 yd	2-1/2 yd	2-1/2 yd
	(1.5m)	(2.25m)	(2.25m)

◆ *Patternmaking supplies:* Paper for making a pattern, pencils and eraser, straight edge or ruler, tailor's chalk or fabric marking pencils, measuring tape, scissors, and pins.

◆ *1-1/8 yd (1m) of elastic gathering tape,* like Stitch & Stretch

◆ *1/2" (1.3 cm) elastic* if you are making fitted sleeves

◆ *9" (23cm) fusible knit or woven medium-weight interfacing* if you want to finish the neck edge of a flannel gown with facing.

◆ *Matching thread.* Decorative thread, if you wish to embellish with decorative stitches.

◆ *Lace, eyelet or other trim* to edge the neckline, sleeves, armhole openings, or hem.

◆ *Decorative bows, rosettes, or buttons.*

PREPARE YOUR FABRIC

Follow instructions on page 5 to wash and dry, or dryclean, your fabric prior to cutting.

CREATE GOWN PATTERN PIECES AND CUT FABRIC

1 Choose the style you want to make. Since these garments are very generous, they comfortably fit large-sized figures.

2 Take your measurements to determine what size you need. If you're in doubt, refer to the section on shaping fabric to fit you on page 7.

3 To create your pattern shapes, refer to the instructions in the section on patterns made of squares and rectangles on page 4, and the illustration Pattern Shape for Adult's Gown, Style #1, and Pattern Shape for Child's Gown, Style #2.

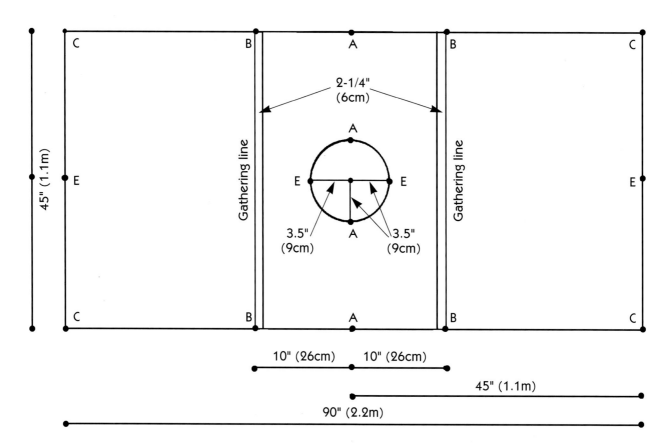

Pattern shape for adult's gown, style #1, size 1/2

• • • ideas • • •

◆ Add sleeves by using the pattern from the Classic Blouse and Turtleneck Top on page 22.

◆ To make a warmer gown, use cotton flannel or a heavier knit and add sleeves gathered into an elastic band.

◆ The wider you cut the gown, the more swirl you get, but remember that full skirts require lighter-weight fabrics. A good rule of thumb for fabric weight is: the heavier the fabric, the fewer the gathers and the slimmer the shape.

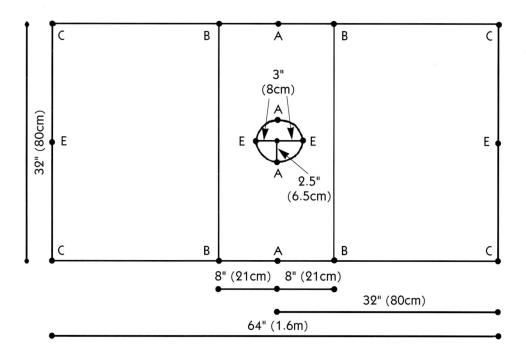

Pattern shape for child's gown, style #2, size medium

4 Use the fabric layout in the illustration Fabric Layout for Gowns. Pin the pattern shapes on the fabric as follows:

a. Fold fabric in half lengthwise.

b. Fold pattern pieces in half lengthwise (along points E).

c. Place center front and back (points E) along fold of fabric.

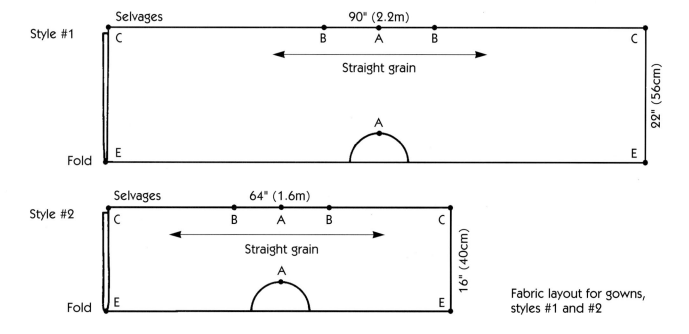

Fabric layout for gowns, styles #1 and #2

5 Cut the fabric using scissors or rotary cutter and mat.

6 Mark alphabet points with tailor's chalk or fabric markers.

CONSTRUCT YOUR SWIRLING GOWN

Bodice of Style #1

1 Serge or sew front and back center seams, if you had to piece them for extra width. Press sewn seams open, and serged seams towards side seams.

2 Finish neck edge by serging or using a zigzag stitch. If you want a lace or eyelet edge, stitch it down on top of the finished neck edge. Otherwise, press neck edge under 1/2" (1.3cm) and topstitch on the outside of the garment. You can also finish raw neck edge with binding and then add decorative trim over it, or sew down the decorative trim and then finish neck edge with binding.

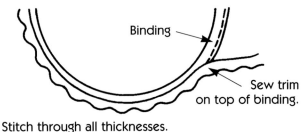

Neck edge trims for gown

3 Pin gathering tape along front and back at points B.

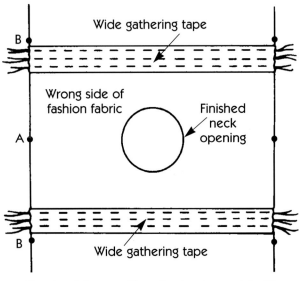

Shaping fullness with gathering tape, style #1

4 Sew tape in place according to manufacturer's instructions.

5 Pull elastic cords until the width of the bodice fits comfortably across your chest in the area between shoulder and bottom of armhole (points A and C). Securely topstitch or zigzag edge of tape at side seams to secure position of elastic. Cut off excess elastic cords.

Bodice of Style #2

1 Pin gathering tape along shoulder line on the wrong side, from the center of point A to point A at neck.

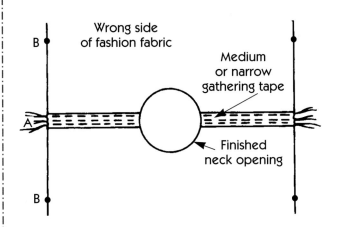

Shaping fullness with gathering tape, style #2

2 Sew tape in place according to manufacturer's instructions.

3 Finish neck edge using a facing or a binding. If you want a lace or eyelet edge, baste it around the neck edge on the outside of the garment first. Pin facing or binding in place over the decorative trim. Sew in place through all thicknesses.

4 At armhole edge pull elastic cording in gathering tape until the shoulder is the width you want. Securely topstitch or zigzag in place at armhole edge and trim off excess elastic cording.

5 Finish armhole to match neck opening.

Side seams and hems for adult's and child's gowns

1 Sew or serge side seams, matching underarm seams at point C, and hemline at point D.

2 Press sewn side seams open, or serged seams to one side.

3 Since this is a full, floaty garment, try it on to make sure the hem hangs evenly. Make necessary adjustments.

4 Turn hem under 1/4" (6mm), press, turn under another 2" (5cm), press, then sew in place. You can blind-hem, topstitch, serge the edge, or hand-hem.

FINISHING TOUCHES

If you want buttons or bows, now is the time to add them. Sew a ribbon, lace or eyelet trim over the serged edges. If you use a turned under hem, add decorative trim wherever you want around the hemline. After you've treated yourself to one of these floaty, feminine gowns, make one as a great gift for a friend or family member.

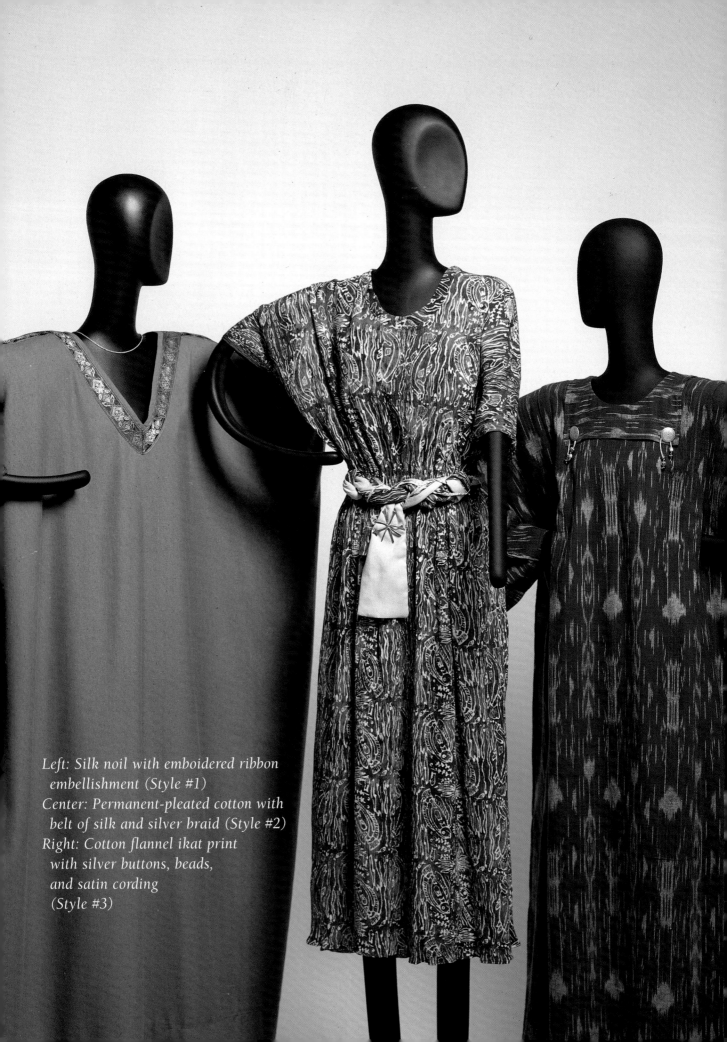

*Left: Silk noil with emboidered ribbon
embellishment (Style #1)*
*Center: Permanent-pleated cotton with
belt of silk and silver braid (Style #2)*
*Right: Cotton flannel ikat print
with silver buttons, beads,
and satin cording
(Style #3)*

Chapter Seven

Caftan Robe & Dress

Do you need a cozy robe for cold winter evenings? Or a pretty gown to slip into on weekend mornings or when friends come over? Pair a flattering, soft fabric with a simple, flowing shape, and you can make a gorgeous caftan robe or casual wear gown in a few hours. This design is actually a reincarnation of the Timeless Top in Chapter Two with the hem dropped to the ankles or below the knees. Instead of shaping the fabric, you let it hang loose and free. You can also use the easy-to-make caftan shape to create a flattering dress. Get out your holiday or birthday gift list and see how many people would love one of these projects. These garments use the full width of 45" (1.1m) fabric, making them more than 72" (1.8m) around which is very generous. They comfortably fit large-sized figures.

PROJECTS

The summer version, Style #1, uses lightweight fabrics that are soft and gentle next to your skin: cotton (woven or knit), cotton/synthetic blends, silks, and rayons are good choices. The emerald green gown is silk noil that can be casual or dressy.

The caftan dress, Style #2, is made of permanently pleated gauze cotton, a perfect fabric for flattering almost any figure.

The warmer winter robe, Style #3, is in wonderfully soft flannel. It would also be attractive in velour, lightweight sweatshirt fleece, or heavyweight knits.

TIPS FOR PLANNING YOUR CAFTAN

You can sew, serge, or fuse this garment together. Remember to consult the list of appropriate fabrics for fusing on page 6 if you choose to fuse all or part of your caftan. You'll need to use a round neckline. Avoid fabrics with one way designs since you won't be able to match the designs at the side seams. Rule of thumb is that heavier fabrics are stiffer, so stick to light or medium weights that drape well.

WHAT TO BUY

◆ *Fabric:* The following fabric requirements for the caftan and dress are for one-size-fits-almost-all, using 45" (1.1m) fabric. The caftan robe is 54" (1.4m) long (ankle length). The dress is 48" (1.2m) long. Their sleeves end just above the wrist. The sleeveless styles drop off the shoulder to above the elbow.

Fabric Chart

Caftan Robe 3 yds (2.75m)

Dress 2-2/3 yds (2.5m)

◆ *Patternmaking supplies:* Paper for making a pattern, pencils and eraser, straight edge or ruler, tailor's chalk or fabric marking pencils, measuring tape, scissors and pins.

◆ *Wide elastic gathering tape* such as Stitch & Stretch

◆ *1/2" (1.3cm) elastic* if you're making fitted sleeves

◆ *1/4 yd (23cm) fusible knit or woven medium-weight interfacing* if you want to finish the neck edge of a flannel robe or dress with facing

◆ *Matching thread. Metallic or other decorative thread* for machine stitched decoration.

◆ *Paper-backed fusible tape* if you want to fuse the garment together.

◆ *Trim, buttons, or other embellishments* to edge the neckline, sleeves, armhole openings, or hem.

Prepare Your Fabric

Follow instructions on page 5 to wash and dry, or dryclean, your fabric prior to cutting.

Create Caftan Pattern Pieces and Cut the Fabric

1 Choose the style you want to make.

2 Take your measurements to determine what size you need. If you're in doubt, refer to the section on shaping fabric to fit you on page 7.

3 To create your pattern shapes, refer to the instructions in the section on patterns made of squares and rectangles, page 4. Also refer to the illustrations Pattern Shapes for Summer Caftan and Dress, Styles #1 and #2, and Pattern Shapes for Winter Caftan, Style #3.

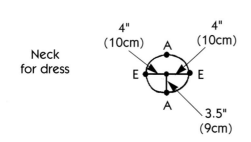

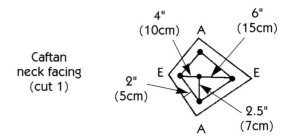

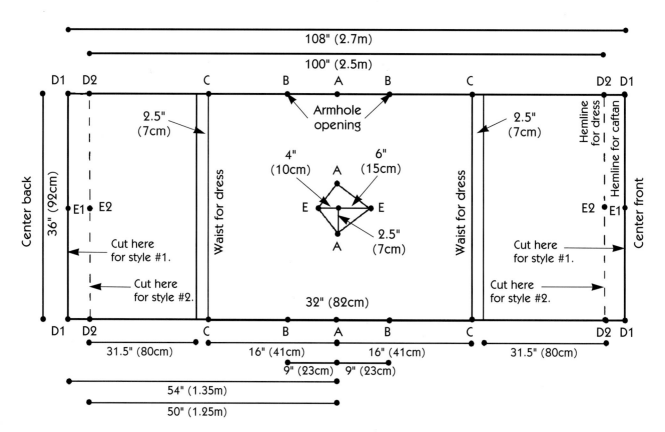

Pattern shapes for summer caftan and dress, styles #1 and #2

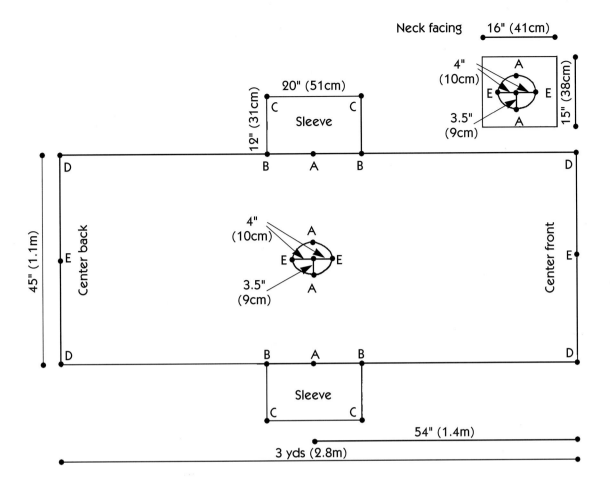

Neck facing 16" (41cm)

4" (10cm)

3.5" (9cm)

15" (38cm)

20" (51cm)

Sleeve

C   C

12" (31cm)

D   D

B   A   B

4" (10cm)

A

E   E

A

3.5" (9cm)

Center back

45" (1.1m)

E   E   Center front

D   D

B   A   B

Sleeve

C   C

54" (1.4m)

3 yds (2.8m)

Pattern shapes for winter caftan, style #3.

4 Use the fabric layout in the illustration Fabric Layout for Caftans. Pin the pattern shapes on the fabric as follows:

   a. Fold fabric in half lengthwise.

   b. Fold pattern pieces in half lengthwise (along points E). Do not fold sleeves pattern.

c. Place center front and back (points E) along fold of fabric. Place sleeve edge against fold.

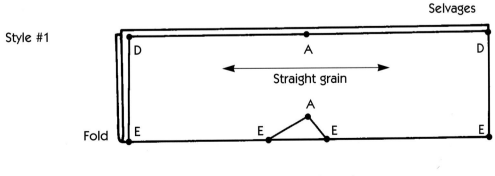

Selvages

Style #1

D   A   D

Straight grain

A

Fold E   E   E   E

Fabric layout for caftans

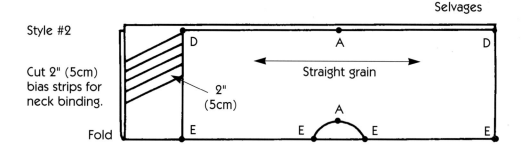

Style #2

Cut 2" (5cm) bias strips for neck binding.

2" (5cm)

Selvages

D   A   D

Straight grain

A

Fold   E   E   E   E

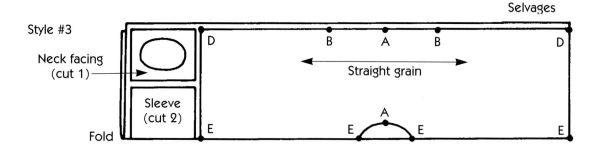

Style #3

Neck facing (cut 1)

Sleeve (cut 2)

Selvages

D   B   A   B   D

Straight grain

A

Fold   E   E   E   E

Fabric layout for caftans

5 Cut the fabric using scissors or rotary cutter and mat. Cut neck facing from single layer. Note that for Style #2 you need 2" (5cm) bias strips that you have to piece together for neck binding.

6 Mark alphabet points with tailor's chalk or fabric markers.

CONSTRUCT YOUR CAFTAN ROBE OR DRESS

Neck and shoulders

1 Finish neck edge with a facing, binding, or by fusing. See page 5 for instructions for neckline finishes.

2 To use the facing decoratively, like the pictured flannel caftan, pin right side of facing to wrong side of fashion fabric at the garment neck edge. Sew, serge, or fuse.

3 Press the seam open, then turn the facing to the outside, press in place, and topstitch or tack down with buttons, rosettes, or beads.

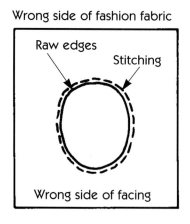

Wrong side of fashion fabric

Raw edges

Stitching

Wrong side of facing

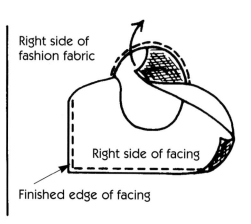

Right side of fashion fabric

Right side of facing

Finished edge of facing

Use facing decoratively.

Armholes or sleeves

1 If you are making the long-sleeved caftan, sew sleeves to armhole openings, matching points B and C.

2 Press seam towards sleeve.

3 Trim excess from edge.

Gathered waist of dress

1 To create the gathered waistline for the dress, sew 2-1/4" (6cm) wide elastic gathering tape along front and back waistline, at points C. See the section on shaping fabric to fit you on page 7 for more information.

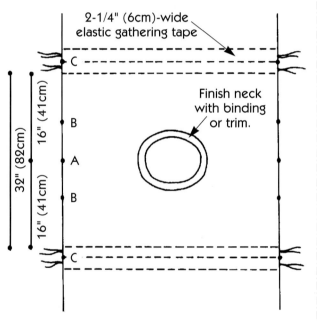

2-1/4" (6cm)-wide elastic gathering tape

Finish neck with binding or trim.

C

B

A

B

C

16" (41cm) 16" (41cm)

32" (82cm)

Create gathered waistband to shape dress.

2 Pull elastic cords of gathering tape until the waistline fits.

3 Secure elastic cords by topstitching or zigzagging several times through tape close to the side edge.

Side seams and hem

1 Sew or serge side seams, matching underarm seams at point B, waistline at C, and hemline at point D.

2 Press sewn side seams open, or to one side.

3 If you're fusing, follow the instructions for the fused Timeless Top in Chapter Two.

4 Turn hem under 1/4" (6mm), press. You can fuse it in place, or turn under another 2" (5 cm), press, and sew. Use a blindhem, topstitch, or hand-hem. If you're using permanently pleated fabric, make a rolled hem, or serge the edges and turn up a narrow hem.

FINISHING TOUCHES

Now is the time to add appliqués, painted motifs, contrasting braid or ribbon trim. If you've made a fancy caftan gown or dress, feel glamorous wearing it to a party or a special occasion like going to the symphony. If you've made the cozy robe, settle down for an evening of comfort.

ideas

- ◆ To make a warmer gown, use warmer fabric, make the sleeves longer, and gather them.
- ◆ Widen the caftan sleeves slightly at the bottom for a more dramatic, flowing look.
- ◆ Try ancient Greek, Egyptian, or other ethnic designs in paint, ribbon, cording, braid, or machine stitching around the front neck edge of the caftan.
- ◆ Use a dramatic print for the dress since its simple lines can carry boldness. If you have access to handwoven fabric, this is a good style for an art-to-wear garment.
- ◆ Vary the width of the garment by choosing wider or narrower fabric.

*Left: Cotton knit with handwoven fabric
 appliqués and matching braid trim
 (Style #2)*
*Right: Reversible fabric of wool/nylon
 blend with one side brushed (Style #1)*

Chapter Eight

Easiest Winter Coat & Summer Wrap

If the poncho is the world's simplest top, the ruana wrap is the world's easiest coat. It's made from one piece of fabric cut up the center front from hem to neck. If you're after winter warmth, stitch the sides closed, leaving an arm opening, and sew a scarf around the neck. Voila! In several hours you have a cozy, attractive cloak. Once you discover how easy the ruana is to make, you'll have fun using this handy design to delight your family and friends.

Projects

The photographed models show how versatile this garment is. The cozy winter coat, Style #1, is made of thick wool blend. The simple cotton knit summer wrap, Style #2, becomes a striking garment with handwoven fabric appliqués.

Tips for Planning Your Wrap

You can fuse, serge, or sew this wrap together, depending on the design and fabric. Here are some guidelines to help you choose:

◆ If you want to fuse the wrap, you'll need to choose one of the fusible fabrics listed on page 6. You'll also need to keep the design simple by not closing side seams and finishing the center and side edges with trim. If you're after warmth, use Velcro glue to add Velcro tab closures.

◆ If you want to serge the wrap, you can use just about any fabric except one with a loose or open weave. Depending on your fabric and design, you can finish the edges with decorative stitching, use your sewing machine to add a scarf or neck band, or stitch or glue pretty trim on the turned edges.

◆ If you want to sew the wrap, you can use just about any fabric, from suede cloth to microfibers, as long as it drapes softly.

What to Buy

◆ *Fabric:* It's very easy to figure out how much 45" (1.1m)-wide fabric you need. If you don't mind a seam up the back, you can work with narrower fabrics. Referring to the illustration and to the measurements section on page 2 in Chapter One, take your shoulder to hem measurement. Double the number and add 2" (5cm) hem allowance. If you want to add a scarf, add 1/4 yd (23cm) more fabric.

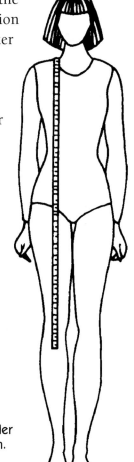

Place tape at shoulder and measure to hem.

If your fabric is very wide [60" (1.5m)] or if you are making a wrap for a child, you won't need extra fabric to add in the scarf.

The finished lengths are 50" (1.25m) for the wool coat and 40" (1m) for the summer wrap. If you want your garment shorter or longer, adjust the amount of fabric you buy accordingly. If you want a lined wrap, purchase the same amount for lining.

Fabric Chart

Winter coat with scarf, Style #1 3-1/2 yd (3.2m)

Summer wrap, Style #2 2-2/3 yd (2.5m)

◆ *Patternmaking supplies:* Paper, pencils and erasers, straight edge or ruler, scissors and pins.

◆ *Matching thread*

◆ *Optional closures* like buttons, Velcro® hook and loop tape, frogs, toggles, or ribbons. If you're fusing, get fusing tape and Velcro glue for optional Velcro tab closures.

◆ *Braid, trim, beads, buttons or any other embellishment.* If you want to finish the edges with decorative binding, such as satin double-fold bias binding, measure the edges for amount to purchase.

PREPARE YOUR FABRIC

Follow instructions on page 5 to wash and dry, or dryclean, your fabric prior to cutting.

CREATE COAT AND WRAP PATTERN PIECES AND CUT FABRIC

1 Choose the style you want to make.

2 Take your measurements to determine the length you need. If you're in doubt, refer to the section on shaping fabric to fit you on page 7.

3 To create your pattern shapes, refer to the instructions in the section on patterns made of squares and rectangles, page 4. Also refer to the illustration Pattern Shapes for Winter Coat, Style #1 and Summer Wrap, Style #2.

NOTE:

◆ Remember to figure in the neckline finish. If you're sewing on binding, you'll have the additional width of a 2" (5cm) binding around the neck and center fronts. You may wish to trim away more of the neck edge and front if you don't want a collar that sticks up.

◆ ◆ ◆ ◆ i d e a s ◆ ◆ ◆ ◆

◆ Add buttons or a belt to keep your wrap closed.

◆ Make a ruana in soft fleece to throw around your shoulders on winter evenings.

◆ Take a beach towel and turn it into an instant beach or pool wrap for a child, or yourself.

◆ Coordinate your wrap with an outfit. For example, choose a dressy silk, cut the hem line in soft curves, and add decorative embellishments.

◆ Use nylon parachute fabric to create a raincape with a scarf wide enough to serve as a hood.

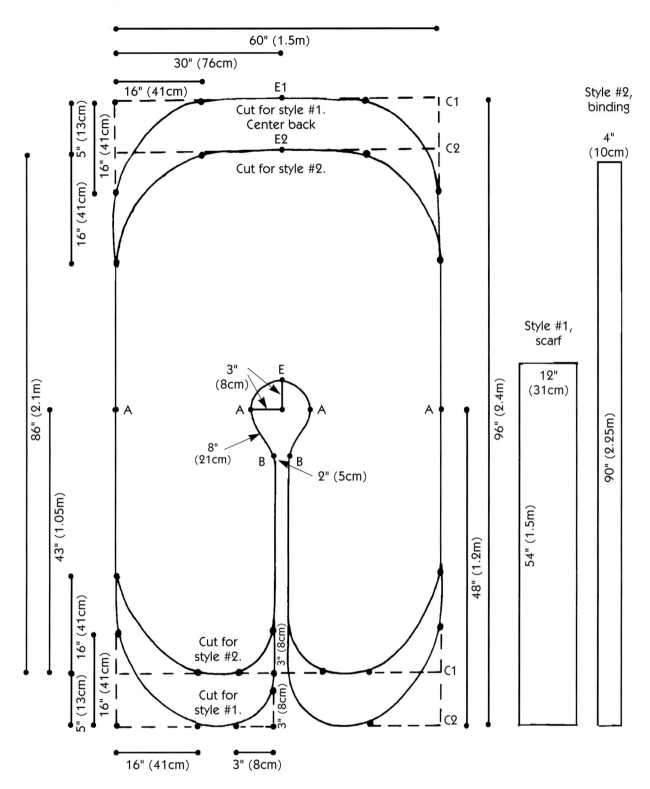

60" (1.5m)

30" (76cm)

16" (41cm)

5" (13cm)

16" (41cm)

16" (41cm)

86" (2.1m)

43" (1.05m)

5" (13cm)

16" (41cm)

16" (41cm)

16" (41cm)

3" (8cm)

E1

Cut for style #1.
Center back

E2

Cut for style #2.

C1

C2

Style #2,
binding

4"
(10cm)

90" (2.25m)

Style #1,
scarf

12"
(31cm)

54" (1.5m)

96" (2.4m)

48" (1.2m)

3"
(8cm)

E

A

A

A

A

8"
(21cm)

B   B

2" (5cm)

Cut for
style #2.

Cut for
style #1.

3" (8cm)

3" (8cm)

C1

C2

Pattern shapes for winter coat, style #1, and summer wrap, style #2

4 Use the fabric layout in the illustration Fabric Layout for Winter Coat, Style #1, and Summer Wrap, Style #2. Pin the pattern shapes on the fabric as follows:

a. Fold fabric in half lengthwise.

b. Fold pattern pieces in half lengthwise (along points E).

c. Place center front and back (points E) along fold of fabric.

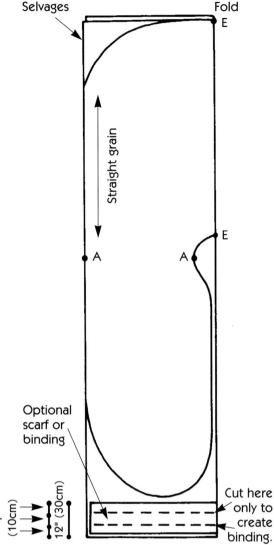

Selvages ←

Fold

E

Straight grain

A

A

E

Optional
scarf or
binding

4" (10cm)

12" (30cm)

Cut here
only to
create
binding.

Fabric layout for winter coat, style #1,
and summer wrap, style #2

NOTE:

◆ Those of you who are confident and
experienced at cutting out patterns may
want to make patterns for the neck,
optional scarf, and side hem curves, and
draw the rest of the body pattern
directly on your fabric in chalk.

5 Cut the fabric using scissors or rotary
cutter and mat.

6 Mark alphabet points with tailor's chalk
or fabric markers.

CONSTRUCT YOUR COAT OR WRAP

Neckline

1 Finish the neckline and front opening. If
you have ravelly, stretchy fabric,

staystitch or baste close to the edge of the
neckline so it will keep its shape.

2 Use whatever method you've chosen to
finish the neck and center front opening:

Sew:

Right sides together, sew on binding. Turn
unsewn edge under 1/4" (6mm), press, and
topstitch. If you have reversible fabric, turn
fabric edge under 1/4" (6mm) and press.
Turn again 1/2" (1.3cm) and press.
Edgestitch in place.

Serge:

Serge the edge, turn it under, press, and
topstitch.

Fuse:

Turn the edge to the outside, fuse it in
place and cover the edge
with glued-on trim.

Right side
of wrap

Decorative trim

Wrong side
of wrap edge

Fusible tape

Fusing neck edges

3 Attach optional scarf at neck edge. If
you are adding the scarf, pin it in place
with wrong sides together, matching center
backs at point A on the neckline. Sew with a
flat-fell or French seam, or serge. Finish the
outer edges of scarf with a rolled or narrow
hem. You can topstitch or hand-hem. Fringe
or hem the bottom edges.

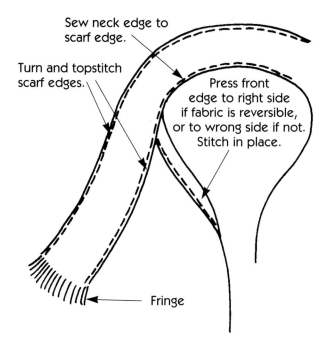

Sew neck edge to scarf edge.

Turn and topstitch scarf edges.

Press front edge to right side if fabric is reversible, or to wrong side if not. Stitch in place.

Fringe

Finishing neck edge and scarf, style #1

Side edges

1 If you want to close the side seams, fold the wrap, right sides together, at point A, the shoulder line. Stitch up from the hem to 10" (25.5cm) from point B. This creates the arm opening. You can make it smaller or larger.

2 Finish the edges of the arm openings with binding. Or make a narrow hem by turning edge under 1/4" (6mm). Press. Turn under another 1/4" (6mm), press, and stitch or fuse in place.

3 If you are leaving the side edges open, finish them with narrow hems, as described in step 2.

Hem

1 Turn the bottom hem edge 1/4" (6mm), and press.

2 Turn the pressed edge under 2" (5cm), and press again.

3 Hand-stitch, topstitch, or fuse in place.

FINISHING TOUCHES

Combine with the gathered skirt in Chapter Four, the Sure-Fit pants in Chapter Ten, or the sarong skirt in Chapter Twelve for a stunning outfit. Add embellishments and enjoy wearing your beautiful new wrap.

Overleaf:
Clockwise from top: Cotton twill fabric with ribbon fused onto edges and belt (Style #1); reversible cotton with damask on solid side and batik on printed side, embellished with satin stitch, pearl buttons and tassels of embroidery floss (Style #2); raw silk with grosgrain ribbon, cording, and braid embellishments (Style #3)

Chapter Nine

One-Hour Vest

Vests are a popular garment for good reason—they go many places and serve many purposes, from dressing up an outfit or giving last year's skirt a fresh look, to keeping you warm. Here's a way to make one in an hour. A fancy or lined vest may take several hours, but you can still make it in an evening.

PROJECTS

This chapter shows how to make a no-sew vest, Style #1; a generous-sized woman's tunic-vest, Style #2; a wearable-art bolero vest, Style #3; and a vest with front closures, Style #4. You'll also find directions for making simple changes in length or width to suit the figure of the wearer.

TIPS FOR PLANNING YOUR VEST

This vest is for anyone and everyone. The length and design details can change to suit your needs. You can fuse, serge, or sew it together, depending on the design you choose and the fabric you use. Avoid fabrics with a nap or one-way design.

◆ If you want to fuse the vest, keep the style loose and flowing, like the long tunic-vest featured and choose one of the fabrics listed on page 6.

◆ If serging is the way you want to go, you can use a wide range of fabrics with the exception of those with a loose or open weave, or stiff, heavy fabric, like thick leather.

◆ If sewing, you can use any of the designs with just about any fabric. The only limitations are how much time you

want to spend making the vest, and how skilled you are with your sewing machine. If you're learning to sew this is a great project for trying new skills and techniques.

WHAT TO BUY

◆ *Fabric:* The following yardage requirements are for 45" (1.1m) fabric. If you want to line your vest, purchase an equal amount of lining fabric.

Fabric Chart

	Child	Adult: 1	2	3	4
Short Vest	1 yd (1m)	1-1/3 yd (1.2m)	1-1/2 yd (1.3m)	1-1/2 yd (1.3m)	1-1/2 yd (1.3m)
Long Vest	1-1/3 yd (1.2m)	1-2/3 yd (1.5m)	1-5/6 yd (1.7m)	1-5/6 yd (1.7m)	1-5/6 yd (1.7m)

◆ *Patternmaking supplies:* Paper for making a pattern, pencils and erasers, straight edge or ruler, tailor's chalk or fabric marking pencils, measuring tape, scissors and pins.

◆ *Matching or contrasting thread* for sewing or serging.

◆ *3/8" (1cm) paper-backed fusible tape* if you're fusing.

◆ *Decorative trim or binding* for neck, armhole openings, and hem.

◆ *Buttons, Velcro® tabs, frogs, toggles, or ribbons* if you want closures.

PREPARE YOUR FABRIC

Follow instructions on page 5 to wash and dry, or dryclean, your fabric prior to cutting.

CREATE VEST PATTERN PIECES AND CUT FABRIC

1 Choose the style you want to make.

2 Take your measurements to determine what size you need. If you're in doubt, refer to the section on shaping fabric to fit you on page 7.

3 To create your pattern shapes, refer to the instructions in the section on patterns made of squares and rectangles, page 4. Also refer to the illustrations for Pattern Shapes for Vests.

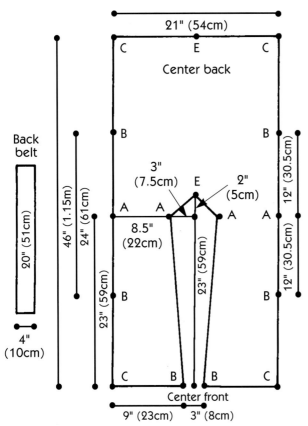

Pattern shape for vest, style #1,
short and loose, size 1

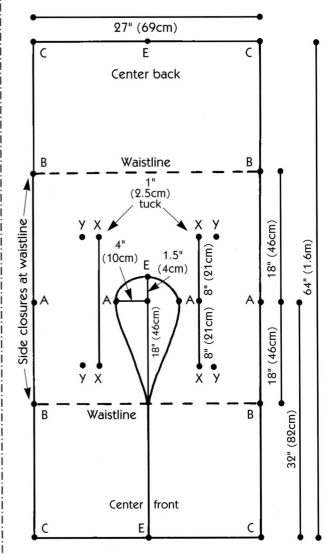

Pattern shape for vest, style #2,
long and loose, generous, size 4

• • • • i d e a s • • • •

◆ Use sweatshirt material or polarfleece and quickly serge a child's warm winter vest.

◆ Use a vest project to help a child or beginning sewer. Even fusing a vest will teach them a lot about working with fabrics.

◆ Appliqué some of your favorite fabric or lace on a vest, or sew on decorative buttons you have been saving for a special project. For lots of exciting ideas for creating pizazz, read *Embellishments: Adding Glamour to Garments* by Linda Fry Kenzle (Chilton Book Company).

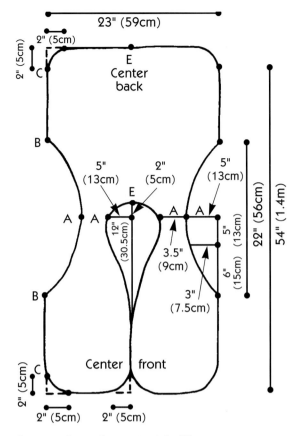

Pattern shape for vest, style #3,
short and fitted, size 2

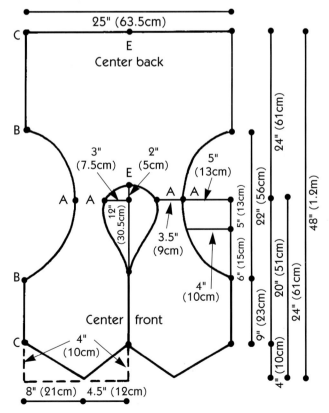

Pattern shape for vest, style #4,
short and fitted, size 3

NOTE:

◆ Remember to figure in the neckline finish. If you're sewing on binding, you'll have the additional width of the binding around the neck and center fronts. You may wish to trim away more of the neck edge and front if you don't want a collar that sticks up.

4 Use the fabric layout in the illustration Fabric Layout for All Vest Styles. Pin the pattern shapes on the fabric as follows:

a. Fold fabric in half lengthwise.

b. Fold pattern pieces in half lengthwise (along points E).

c. Place center front and back (points E) along fold of fabric.

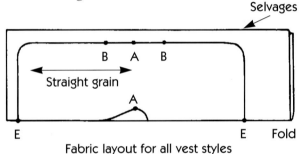

Fabric layout for all vest styles

5 Cut the fabric using scissors or rotary cutter and mat.

6 Mark alphabet points with tailor's chalk or fabric markers.

CONSTRUCT YOUR ONE-HOUR VEST

Neckline and front opening

1 If you have ravelly, stretchy fabric, staystitch or baste close to the edge of the neckline so it will keep its shape.

2 Use one of these finishing techniques:

Sew:

Sew on binding, turn, press, and topstitch in place.

Serge:

Serge the edge, turn it under, press, and topstitch.

Fuse:

Turn 1/2" (1.3cm) at the edge to the outside, and fuse it in place using the clip-and-fit technique as shown in the illustration and outlined on page 7.

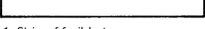

1. Strip of fusible tape

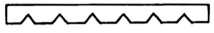

2. Clip tape.

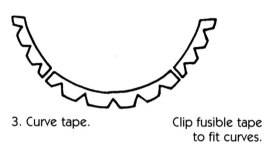

3. Curve tape.   Clip fusible tape to fit curves.

Cover the fused edge by gluing or fusing on trim, or use decorative machine stitching as in the photographed model of Style #2.

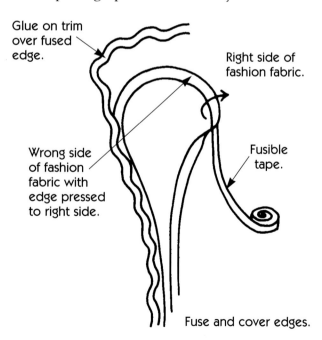

Glue on trim over fused edge.

Right side of fashion fabric.

Wrong side of fashion fabric with edge pressed to right side.

Fusible tape.

Fuse and cover edges.

Side seams for Styles #1, #3, and #4

1 Fold vest at points A, right sides together.

2 Pin the side seams from hem, points C, up to points B, creating arm openings which you can make larger or smaller. Sew, serge, or fuse the seams together.

3 To finish the edges of the arm openings, serge Style #4; on Styles #1 and #3, turn under 1/4" (6mm). Press and turn under another 1/4" (6mm). Press and topstitch, hand-hem, or fuse to inside of fashion fabric.

Side-Slit for Style #2

Sew:

1 Turn under side edges 1/4" (6mm) and press.

2 Turn under another 1/4" (6mm) and press.

3 Topstitch, blind-hem, or hand-hem in place.

Serge:

Overlock side edges with a wide stitch or rolled hem using decorative thread or embroidery floss.

Fuse:

1 Press all the side edges, front and back, 3/8" (1cm) to the outside.

2 Fuse edge to outside using 3/8" (6mm) fusible tape. See page 7 for more details.

3 Glue trim or decorative braid on top of the edges to cover them.

Whatever method you use to finish side seams, hold front and backs together with frogs, buttons and loops, or tabs made of fashion fabric.

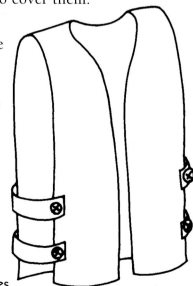

Side closures

Fold vest at points A, place fasteners between points B and C on each side.

Hem

1 Turn up the hem edge 1/4" (6mm) and press.

2 Turn the pressed edge under 2" (10cm) and press again.

3 Hand-hem, topstitch, blindhem, or fuse in place.

Shape Shoulders

If the shoulders need shaping, here are some attractive ways to shape them to your figure:

◆ Add small shoulder pads.

◆ Make tucks at the edges of the shoulders and secure with buttons to create a decorative flap that reduces the armhole fullness. See the section on shaping fabric to fit you on page 7.

◆ Take one or more tucks at least 1" (2.5cm) wide over the shoulders, as shown in the illustration Shaping Tucks for Vest Shoulders.

Glue or sew decorative trim along tuck stitching, or decorative machine stitch along tucks.

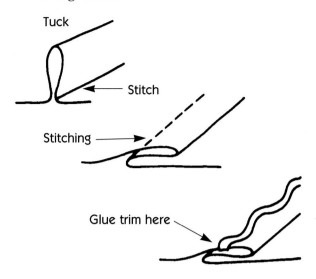

Tuck

Stitch

Stitching

Glue trim here

FINISHING TOUCHES

Combine with the gathered skirt, Chapter Four, the sarong skirt, Chapter Twelve, or the Sure-Fit pants, Chapter Ten. Add whatever embellishment you've planned. Slip on your vest and enjoy the new look.

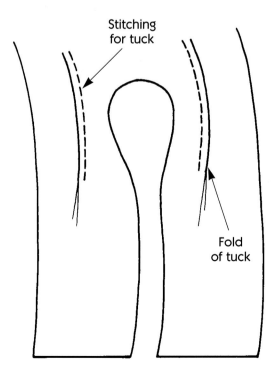

Stitching for tuck

Fold of tuck

Shaping tucks for vest shoulders

Left: Pants (Style #2) in polyester dobby weave, polyester blouse, and belt by Ellen Edith (see cover caption). Right: Black silk noil skirt (Style #1) purchased blouse with button covers.

Sure-Fit Pants & Shorts

Who has not felt their body was not made to wear pants? You try loose-fitting pants because they're comfortable, but they make you feel dumpy. Fitted slacks are just right for your hips, but you're afraid to eat or drink lest the button or zipper pops. Your jeans seemed to fit, but one washing and they're too tight in the crotch. What to do? Try this chapter's ingenious pants from the Indonesian island of Bali.

The glory of Balinese wrap-around pants is that you tie them where they feel best on you, and they fit and flatter a wide variety of body shapes. You can adjust the waistline and crotch height. In hot weather, wear them looser and with less wrap-over. Try them tied in a dramatic knot at the ankle, or leave them long and flowing. You can keep them closed or let them show a flash of leg. They're even easy to slip into and here's how:

1 Fold the pants down the center along the inner leg seams, turning right sides together. You should end up with a U shape with the crotch at the bottom. See the illustration How to Put on Sure-Fit Pants or Shorts.

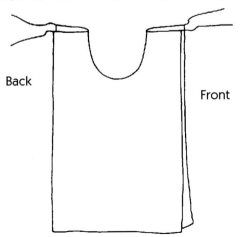

How to put on Sure-Fit pants or shorts

2 Pull the folded pants between your legs.

3 Raise the front and back waistbands to waist level.

4 Open out the back section, bring the ties around your waist to the front, and tie.

5 Spread open the front section over the first ties. Bring the front ties around to the back and tie in a knot or a bow.

6 If you are wearing the long style, try tying the bottom corners in a floppy knot at the ankles.

PROJECTS

The photographed models show some of the endless possibilities for this clever design. Style #1, black, silk noil, knee-length walking shorts, are smart, versatile and comfortable year around. Style #2, the grape, long trousers in a polyester, are elegant as wide-legged palazzo pants, or dramatic knotted at the ankles. Paired with the Classic Blouse from Chapter Three, a purchased belt, and a hand-painted silk vest by artist Joy Stocksdale, they make a striking art-to-wear statement.

TIPS FOR PLANNING YOUR PANTS OR SHORTS

You have lots of options in planning your pants or shorts. They will look wonderful with any type of top. You can make them at any length that suits you. A wide range of light- to medium-weight fabrics are suitable for Balinese trousers: cotton poplin or voile, rayons, linen blends, fine wool, polyester, fine flannel, and silks in a variety of weights.

Avoid fabrics that have a nap, or that are coarse, stiff, loosely woven, or bulky.

You can finish the side edges and hems by fusing, but you'll need to sew or serge the legs and waistband.

WHAT TO BUY

◆ *Fabric:* The following fabric requirements for all sizes are based on 36"-45" (91.5-1.1m)-wide fabric. You also need 1/4 yd (23cm) of lightweight fusible interfacing for the waist ties.

Fabric Chart

Style #1, Short Pants 2 yd (1.85m)

Style #2, Long Pants 2-3/4 yd (2.61m)

◆ *Patternmaking supplies:* Paper for making a pattern, pencils and eraser, straight edge or ruler, tailor's chalk or fabric marking pencils, measuring tape, scissors and pins.

◆ *Thread* to match fabric, or contrast, if you use a decorative stitch.

◆ *1/2" (1.3cm) elastic gathering tape* (optional) to help shape fabric to your waistline.

PREPARE YOUR FABRIC

Follow instructions on page 5 to wash and dry, or dryclean, your fabric prior to cutting.

CREATE PANTS/SHORTS PATTERN AND CUT FABRIC

1 Choose the style you want to make.

2 Take your measurements and select the size you'll make from the following chart. Refer to the section on measuring on page 2 if you need more information. Measure the finished length you want, and add at least 2" (5cm) to that number for finishing the waist and hem. Compare your length against the measurements for finished lengths. Note what adjustment you need to make to the final pattern.

Pants Measurements

	Adult: 1/2	3/4
Waist Size	23-28"	28-33"
	(57-71cm)	(71-84cm)
Hip Size	33-40"	40-48"
	(84-97cm)	(97-110cm)
Finished Length		
Style #1	22"	22"
	(56cm)	(56cm)
Style #2	42"	42"
	(106.5cm)	(106.5cm)

3 To create your pattern shapes, refer to the instructions in the section on patterns made of squares and rectangles, page 4. Also refer to the illustration Pattern Shapes for Sure-Fit Pants and Shorts. Use

♦ ♦ ♦ i d e a s ♦ ♦ ♦

◆ To create a closer fit, add elastic in the waistband.

◆ Try black satin or panne velvet topped off with a white satin Timeless Top for a chic party outfit.

◆ Embellish the pants by adding decorative trim, braid, appliqués, or painted motifs down the outside edges of the legs or along the hem.

◆ Pocket fans can add patch pockets to the front or back, or both. For wonderful ideas on how to use pockets as design statements, read Claire Shaeffer's *Sew Any Patch Pocket* and *Sew Any Set-In Pocket* (Chilton Book Company).

◆ For variety, hem the shorter version with turned up cuffs.

your waist, hip, hem length, and waist-to-crotch measurements to adjust the pattern to suit your figure. For sizes requiring a deeper crotch fitting, simply lower the crotch line on the pattern, keeping the same width and shape.

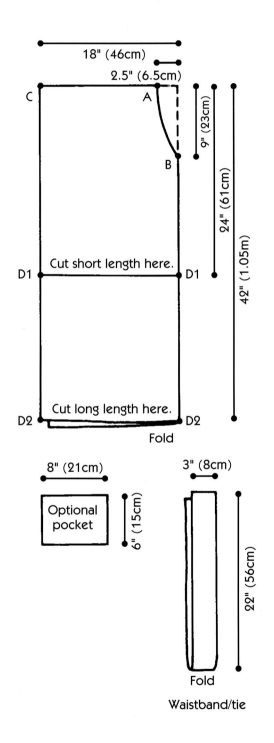

Pattern shapes for Sure-Fit pants and shorts, styles #1 and #2, size 1/2

4 Use the fabric layout in the illustration Fabric Layout for Sure-Fit Pants and Shorts. Pin the pattern shapes on the fabric as follows:

a. Fold fabric in half lengthwise.

b. Fold pattern pieces in half lengthwise (along points E).

c. Place center front and back (points E) along fold of fabric.

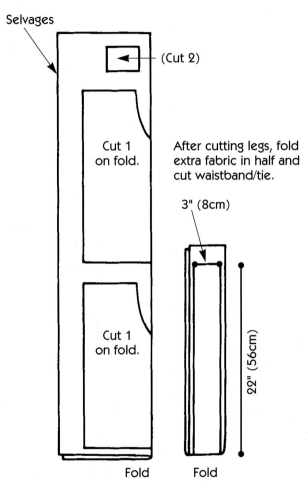

Fabric layout for Sure-Fit pants and shorts

5 Cut the fabric using scissors or rotary cutter and mat.

6 Mark alphabet points with tailor's chalk or fabric markers.

CONSTRUCT YOUR SURE-FIT PANTS OR SHORTS

Side Edges and Hems

1 Start with side edges by either overlocking or by turning in 1/4" (6mm) seam allowance. Press, and turn again 1/4" (6mm). Topstitch with straight, zigzag, or decorative stitch.

2 Finish hems the same way, first overlocking on your serger, or turning 1/4" (6mm). Press, then turn 1-1/4" (3 cm). Press, and topstitch with straight or decorative stitch.

Optional pockets

1 Turn under all edges of patch pocket 1/4" (6mm) and press.

2 Turn under top edge another 1/4" (6mm), press, and topstitch.

3 Pin patch pockets in position on leg pieces. Topstitch, strengthening corners with bar tacks.

Assemble legs

All the leg pieces are the same, so this is easy.

1 Right sides together, pin, then serge or stitch the two leg pieces along the crotch curve.

2 If you're using your sewing machine, reinforce by stitching again along the inside of the curve. Finish the edges by zigzagging.

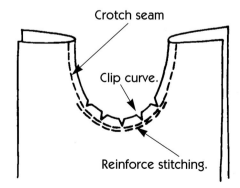

Reinforce crotch curve.

Waistband ties

1 If you're using really lightweight fabric, consider fusing a strip of interfacing onto the middle of each waistband for the length of your waist.

2 Right sides together, pin a waistband to the top of each pant section, making sure to match centers at point A. Stitch with serger or sewing machine.

3 Leave a small opening at each end of the waistband at the side seam edge for inserting elastic if you want to pull in the waist. For instructions turn to the section on shaping fabric to fit (page 7). If you use regular soft elastic, topstitch along the length of the waistband, over the elastic, several times to create a flat, smocking effect. The black walking shorts in the photograph have this "smocked" waistline elastic.

4 Fold each tie end in half lengthwise, right sides together. Pin raw edges of ties up to where the waistband is sewn to the pant leg. Stitch the tie ends with a 1/4" (6mm) seam. Trim corner thickness, turn right sides out, and press.

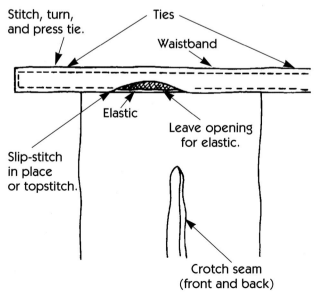

Waistband/tie

5 Press under 1/4" (6mm) of remaining raw edges of waistband/ties along inside of waistband. Pin in place and slip-stitch to inside waist seam, or topstitch along outside edges of waistband/ties. Press.

FINISHING TOUCHES

Embellish with trim down the side edge of the pant leg, on the pocket, or hem, or leave unadorned. Either way, you have a comfortable pair of pants or shorts.

Create a stunning outfit by combining pants or shorts with one or more of these other easy projects: Timeless Top from Chapter Two, Classic Blouse from Chapter Three, Easy Wrap from Chapter Eight, Kimono Coat from Chapter Eleven, or Cocoon from Chapter Thirteen.

Overleaf:
Left: Cotton velour/terry cloth beach towels (Style #2)
Right: Rayon velvet with gold metallic embroidery and
*   polyester satin lining (Style #1)*

Kimono Coat

The Japanese kimono, worn for over a thousand years, is a good example of a traditional design that has become trans-cultural. The Japanese turned their kimonos into an art form, lavishing them with embroidery, dyeing, tie-dyeing, hand-painting, appliqué, stencilling, and block printing. Highly valued designs were subtle and daring, suggesting movement and contrast through bold use of color and pattern. Clothing designers around the world have been inspired by the graceful kimono. Not only does it flatter a wide variety of body shapes, its symmetrical shape and large surface area are ideal for decoration. The design featured in this chapter is a simplified version of the kimono. It has the kimono's ingenious "pocket" sleeves, but it is simple to make, requiring only a few pieces to sew or serge. Choose interesting fabric, and you'll have an unusual, beautiful garment.

PROJECTS

The styles featured in this chapter show that you can use the elegant lines to showcase a special fabric or to combine several fabrics. The deep, dramatic sleeves create pockets, perfect for carrying small items. Make an evening coat, Style #1, and stash your comb, lipstick, and small wallet in the sleeve pocket, or use three beach towels, as in Style #2, to create a beach robe with handy sleeve pockets for sunglasses and sunscreen.

TIPS FOR PLANNING YOUR KIMONO

This beautiful, simple to make wrap can be yours in an afternoon or evening. It's cut the same way for men, women, and children, and it looks great with summer or winter fabrics. In order to keep the design easy enough for beginners to make, I've simplified the front panels and the sleeve. This is not a fusible garment. You'll need to serge, or preferably sew and serge it. If you're lining your kimono, purchase the same amount of lining fabric as fashion fabric. Style #1 is lined, and Style #2 uses beach towels and is unlined.

Fabrics that are soft and lightweight work well. This gives you a wide range of summer and winter fabrics such as cotton lawn, fine poplin, polyester and polyester-cotton blends, silk rayon, fine wool challis, wool-cotton blends, and velvet.

WHAT TO BUY

◆ *Fabric:* The following fabric requirements for all adult sizes are for 45" (1.1m)-wide fabric or specified towels. If you want to line Style #1, buy the same amount of lining.

Fabric Chart

Style #1, Fabric Kimono	4.5 yd (4.1 m)
Style #2, Beach towel kimono	3 bath sheets or large beach towels
Style #2, Child's size	2 bath sheets or large beach towels

This Japanese-inspired one-size garment fits the body measurements that follow. For larger sizes, plan to add extra fabric at the side seams, but the sleeves and collar can remain the same. You also can adjust the hem and sleeve lengths to suit your needs, but make sure you account for any changes when you calculate the amount of fabric you're buying. You may need to buy extra material if you use fabric with a directional pattern such as stripes.

Measurements for One-Size-Fits-Most Kimono

	Chest	Hips	Length
One-size	32-36"	34-38"	50"
	(81-92cm)	(86-97cm)	(1.27m)

◆ *Patternmaking supplies:* Paper for making a pattern, pencils and eraser, straight edge or ruler, tailor's chalk or fabric marking pencils, measuring tape, scissors, and pins.

◆ *Fusible or sew-in interfacing* if you're using lightweight fabric that needs more body for the collar.

◆ *Matching or contrasting thread.*

◆ *Buttons, frogs, or ties* for optional closures

◆ *Embellishments* such as braid, trim, appliqués, beads, and buttons.

◆ ◆ ◆ i d e a s ◆ ◆ ◆

◆ For the feel of pure luxury make a robe out of a silk or polyester satin.

◆ For a graceful, comfortable dress, combine several fabrics into a kimono with buttons or tie closures, and add a belt.

◆ Try combining several different but complementary fabrics as suggested. Keep the straight grain of the different fabrics going in the same vertical direction on the garment. Piece together your different fabrics using the basic pattern shapes.

◆ Leave knee high side slits in the side seams for more ease of movement.

◆ Purchased cord frogs with buttons are striking as closures. For a smooth appearance, sew on small snaps in strategic places if you want to keep your kimono closed.

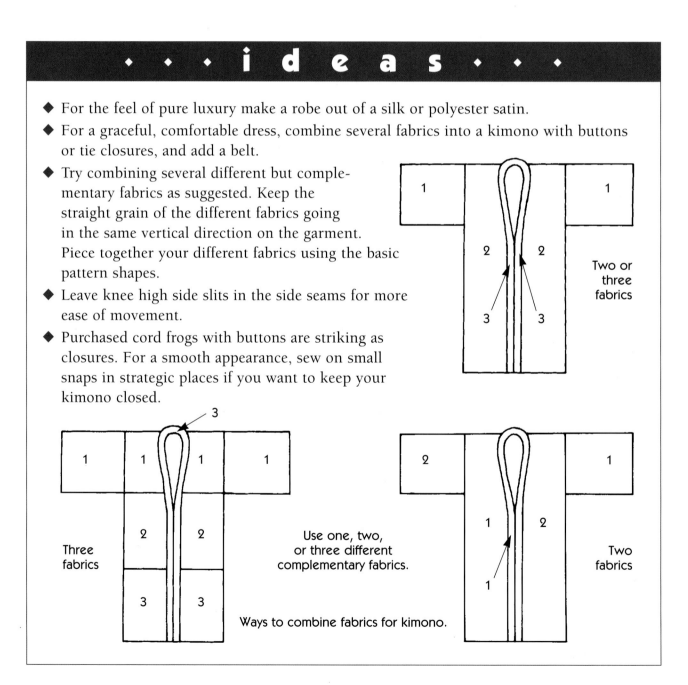

Ways to combine fabrics for kimono.

PREPARE YOUR FABRIC

Follow instructions on page 5 to wash and dry, or dryclean, your fabric prior to cutting.

CREATE KIMONO PATTERN AND CUT FABRIC

1 Choose the style you want to make.

2 Take your measurements to determine if you need to add extra width at the side seams. If you're in doubt, refer to the section on measuring on page 2 and on shaping fabric to fit you on page 7.

3 To create your pattern shapes, refer to the instructions in the section on patterns made of squares and rectangles, page 4. Also refer to the illustration Pattern Shapes for Kimonos. Adjust for your measurements. Note that all seam allowances are 1/2" (1.3cm).

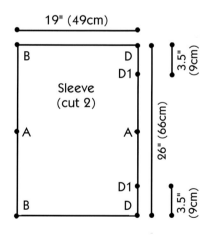

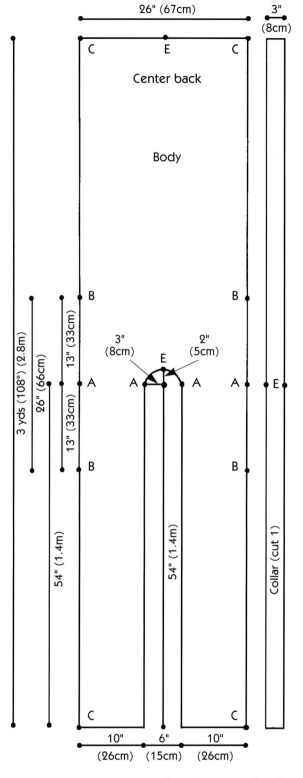

Pattern shapes for kimono, styles #1 and #2

4 Use the fabric layout in the illustration Fabric Layout for Kimono.

Pin the pattern shapes on the fabric as follows:

a. Fold fabric in half lengthwise.

b. Fold pattern pieces in half lengthwise (along points E). Do not fold sleeve pattern. You need 2 sleeves. Also do not fold collar pattern.

c. Place center front and back (points E) along fold of fabric.

d. After cutting body and sleeves, use remaining fabric to cut collar and sash.

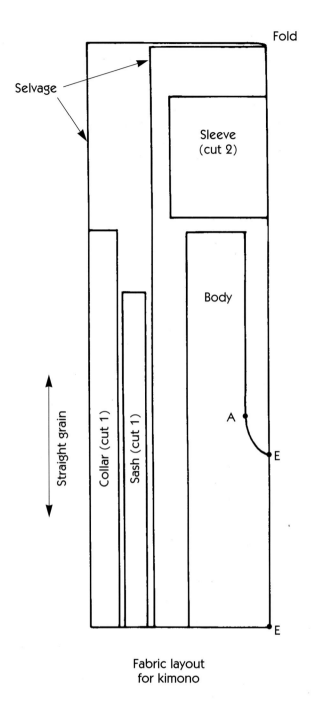

Selvage

Fold

Sleeve (cut 2)

Body

Collar (cut 1)

Sash (cut 1)

Straight grain

A

E

E

Fabric layout
for kimono

5 Cut the fabric using scissors or rotary cutter and mat.

6 Mark alphabet points with tailor's chalk or fabric markers.

CONSTRUCT YOUR UNLINED KIMONO

Add collar and front edging

1 Fuse or baste interfacing to wrong side of collar band, leaving 1/2" (1.3cm) seam allowance.

2 With right sides together, pin collar to kimono body piece. Match center backs at points E. Stitch. Press seam allowance toward front edge.

3 Turn collar hem under 1/4" (6mm). Slip-stitch or topstitch.

4 Turn collar edge under 1/4" (6mm). Press. Starting and stopping about 4" (10cm) from bottom, slip-stitch or topstitch to kimono body, enclosing all raw edges. (Leave collar at hem area unfinished until you have sewn hem— a step that comes later.)

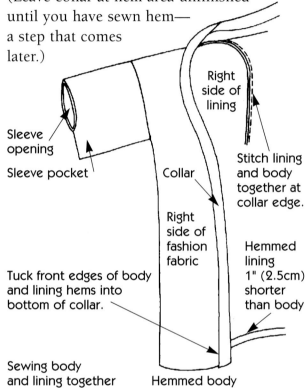

Right side of lining

Stitch lining and body together at collar edge.

Sleeve opening

Sleeve pocket

Collar

Right side of fashion fabric

Hemmed lining 1" (2.5cm) shorter than body

Tuck front edges of body and lining hems into bottom of collar.

Sewing body and lining together

Hemmed body

Attach sleeves

1 Finish raw edges by zigzagging or overlocking.

2 Right sides together, match sleeve centers, points A, to kimono shoulder centers, points A. Stitch from point B on front to point B on back.

Join side seams

1 Right sides together, fold kimono at shoulder points A making hems level. Stitch side seams from sleeve pocket edge, point D through underarm, point B to hem, point C.

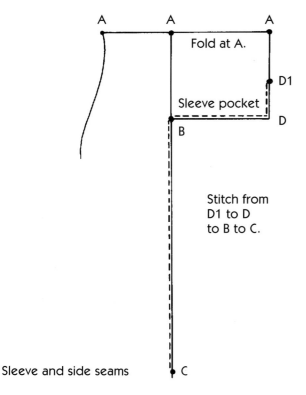

A   A   A

Fold at A.

D1

Sleeve pocket

D

B

Stitch from
D1 to D
to B to C.

Sleeve and side seams   C

2 Finish raw edge at sleeve opening in one of these ways:

Hand-stitch:

Turn under raw edges 1/4" (6mm), press, then turn again and slip-stitch edge to sleeve.

Sew:

Turn under 1/4" (6mm), press, turn under another 1/4" (6mm), press, and top-stitch in place.

Serge:

Since you're not lining your coat, you can serge this edge. Turn it under 1/4" (6mm), and topstitch in place.

Complete hems

1 Turn up bottom hem 3/8" (1cm), then 1–1/2" (4cm) and slip-stitch or machine finish.

2 Tuck front edges of body hem into bottom of collar. Slip-stitch in place. Finish and hem bottom of collar. Press.

Optional sash

1 Right sides together, join sash pieces, leaving one end open. Clip fabric close to corners to reduce bulk.

2 Turn sash right side out and press.

3 Press under 1/4" (6mm) of unfinished end, and stitch turned edges together.

Optional closures

Attach your choice of closures such as frogs, toggles, and other interesting fasteners.

CONSTRUCT YOUR LINED KIMONO

If you're lining your kimono, construct the lining shell, then the coat, leaving collar for last. Follow this order of construction for both the lining shell and the coat:

1 Attach sleeves as for unlined kimono.

2 Join side seams and create sleeve pocket as for unlined kimono.

3 Join coat to lining. Refer to illustration Sewing Body and Lining Together (page 72).

    a. Layer coat over lining, wrong sides together, matching marks and seams.

    b. Stitch together at collar edge in a 1/2" (1.3cm) seam

    c. Press under raw edges of sleeves in lining and fashion fabric. Slip-stitch together by hand.

4 Complete hems. Turn up lining hem 1" (2.5cm) shorter than fashion fabric hem. Sew separately from fashion fabric.

5 Add collar as for unlined kimono. Tuck front edges of body and lining hems into bottom of collar. Slip-stitch in place. Hem bottom of collar.

FINISHING TOUCHES

You have a stunning coat, beach robe, or dress to wear as is or to embellish with stitching, embroidery, beads and jewels, fused on appliqués, or whatever you want. Turn to the books in the Resource List for ideas.

Don't be surprised when your friends ask, "Where did you get that coat? It's gorgeous."

*Left: Sandwashed
silk sarong
(Style #2) with
satin acetate blouse
Right: Rayon print
sarong (Style #1)
with purchased
silk blouse*

Chapter Twelve

Sarong Skirt

For graceful lines, you can't beat one of the world's oldest skirts, the sarong. In recent years this traditional garment, worn by both men and women of Malaysia, Indonesia, and the Pacific Islands, has enjoyed a comeback. And no wonder—its classic shape is comfortable and wearable, yet has a touch of magic.

PROJECTS

This flattering skirt can be yours in two hours. As the models show, a sarong can be worn any length, so choose your favorite hemline. Style #1 shows a short, sun-splashed rayon perfect for casual summer wear. Change gears with Style #2, a long, sandwashed silk to wear to work or to any dress-up event. Measurements are also given for an above-the-calf length.

TIPS FOR PLANNING YOUR SARONG

You can sew, serge and sew, or fuse and sew this skirt together. Try any light- to medium-weight fabric. Just make sure the fabric you select drapes nicely and doesn't have an obvious diagonal pattern. Also avoid material with pile or one-way designs unless you know how to lay out and cut these special fabrics.

WHAT TO BUY

- *Fabric:* Using 45" (1.1m)-wide fabric, you need the same fabric requirements for all adult sizes:

Fabric Chart

Above Knee	1-2/3 yd (1.5m)
Above Calf	1-2/3 yd (1.5m)
Below Calf	1-2/3 yd (1.5m)

- *Patternmaking supplies:* Paper for the pattern, pencils and eraser, straight edge or ruler, tailor's chalk or fabric marking pens, scissors and pins.
- *Matching or contrasting thread*
- *Two 5/8" (1.5cm) buttons or Velcro® tabs along with Velcro glue for closures*
- *18" (46cm) waistband elastic*

PREPARE YOUR FABRIC

Follow instructions on page 5 to wash and dry, or dryclean, your fabric prior to cutting.

CREATE SARONG PATTERN AND CUT FABRIC

1 Choose the style you want to make.

2 Take your measurements and select the size and length you'll make from the following chart. Sizes are included here for your convenience. Refer to the section on measuring on page 2 if you need more information.

Sarong and Body Measurements

	Adult:		
	1	2	3
Waist	22-26"	27-28"	29-30"
	(56-66cm)	(67-71cm)	(72-76cm)
Hip	32-36"	37-40"	41-44"
	(81-92cm)	(93-102cm)	(103-112cm)
Sarong Length			
Style #1	21"	24"	25"
Above Knee	(54cm)	(61cm)	(64cm)
Above Calf	26"	28"	28"
	(66cm)	(71cm)	(71cm)
Style #2	30"	38"	38"
Below Calf	(76cm)	(96.5cm)	(96.5cm)

3 To create your pattern shapes, refer to the section on patterns made of squares and rectangles, page 4. Also refer to the illustration Pattern Shapes for Sarong, Styles #1 and #2. Adjust for your measurements. Note that all seam allowances are 1/2" (1.3cm).

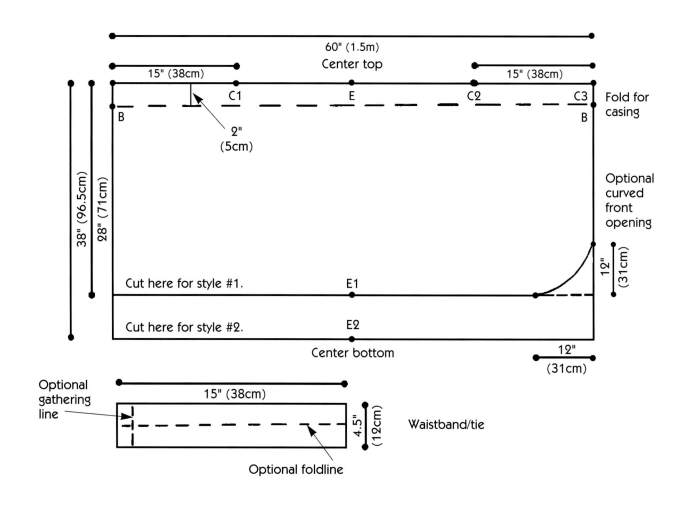

Pattern shapes for sarong, styles #1 and #2, size 2

◆ Use satin, a dressy silk, or panne velvet and the sarong reincarnates as a perfect skirt for a dressy occasion.

◆ Use a cool weave cotton or lightweight cotton knit for a comfortable hot weather cover up.

◆ If you want an exotic, tropical look use batik fabric. See the Resource List for sources of unusual or ethnic fabrics.

4 Use the fabric layout in the illustration Fabric Layout for Sarong, Styles #1 and #2.

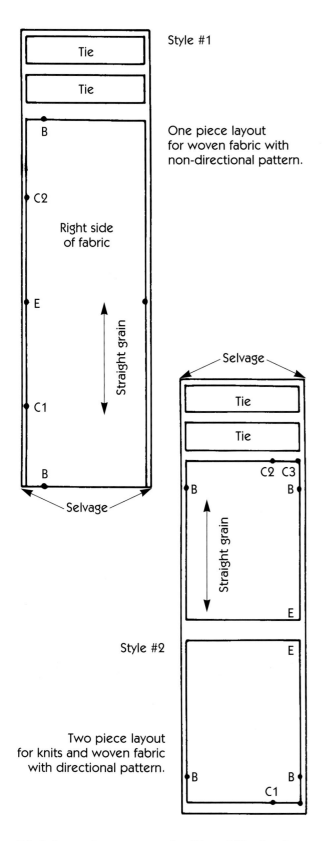

Style #1

One piece layout for woven fabric with non-directional pattern.

Right side of fabric

Straight grain

Style #2

Two piece layout for knits and woven fabric with directional pattern.

Fabric layout for sarong, styles #1 and #2, size 2

Pin the pattern shapes on the fabric as follows:

a. Fold fabric in half lengthwise.

b. Fold pattern pieces in half lengthwise (along points E).

c. Place center front and back (points E) along fold of fabric.

NOTE:

The two-piece layout is only for knits and woven fabrics with a vertical direction pattern. It requires cutting two panels instead of one and then sewing a seam.

5 Cut the fabric using scissors or rotary cutter and mat.

6 Mark alphabet points with tailor's chalk or fabric markers.

CONSTRUCT YOUR SARONG

Whether you sew, sew and serge, or sew and fuse your garment together, follow this order of construction.

Finish side edges

1 Right sides together, pin panels together (if you needed to make panels). Sew or serge a 1/2" (1.3cm) seam and press.

2 Choose one of these methods to finish edges:

Sew:

Turn side edges under 1/4" (6mm) and press. Turn under another 1/4" (6mm), press. Topstitch.

Serge:

Overlock all edges of fabric.

Fuse:

Press paper-backed 3/8" (1cm) fusible tape along raw side edges. Peel off paper, turn, and fuse in place.

Waistband

1 Finish waistband with one of these methods:

Sew:

Turn raw edges under 1/4" (6mm) and press.

Serge:

Overlock all edges of fabric.

Fuse:

Press paper-backed 3/8" (1cm) fusible tape along raw edges. Peel off paper, turn, and fuse in place.

2 Turn finished edge of waistband wrong sides together to create a 2-1/2" (7cm) casing. Topstitch, leaving a 3" (8cm) opening at the center back for inserting elastic.

Fold over top of waist to create a 2" waistband.

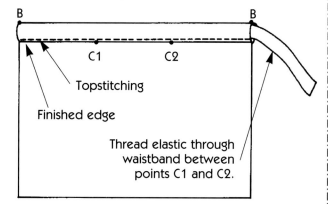

Waistband

3 Cut waistband elastic to fit your waistline at the back. Put the elastic in casing at the center back so that it lies between points C1 and C2. Stitch to secure each end of the elastic. If you have regular, soft elastic, topstitch several rows along the length of the elastic to create a smocking effect. Stitch to close the 3" (8cm) opening in center back casing.

Ties

1 Make two ties, using one of these methods:

   ◆ *Turned tube tie:* Right sides together, sew tie on three sides, turn right side out, and press flat.

   ◆ *Gathered tie with finished edges:* Serge three edges of tie. To sew, turn

three edges under 1/4" (6mm), press. Turn under another 1/4" (6mm), press, and topstitch. Gather or make pleats on unfinished end so tie end is 2" (5cm) wide.

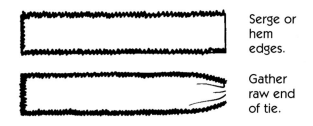

Serge or hem edges.

Gather raw end of tie.

2 Insert raw end of one tie into opening at end of waistband at point C3, turning under raw edge of waistband. Topstitch.

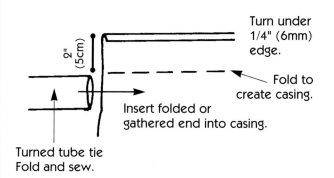

Turn under 1/4" (6mm) edge.

Fold to create casing.

Insert folded or gathered end into casing.

Turned tube tie
Fold and sew.

3 Turn under raw end of other tie, place across end of elastic at C1, and topstitch.

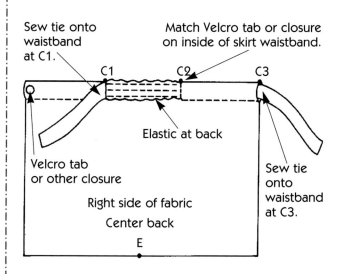

Sew tie onto waistband at C1.

Match Velcro tab or closure on inside of skirt waistband.

Elastic at back

Velcro tab or other closure

Sew tie onto waistband at C3.

Right side of fabric
Center back

Sew ties onto waistband.

Hem and closures

1 Straighten hem if needed. Turn hem edge up 1/4" (6mm) and press. If you've already serged the edge you can omit this step.

2 Turn hem edge under another 1" (2.5cm) and press.

3 Topstitch, machine-hem, hand-hem, or fuse in place.

4 Stitch on Velcro® tabs, sew snaps, or add a button and make a buttonhole, to keep left end of sarong wrapped around your body on the inside of the skirt.

FINISHING TOUCHES

This skirt is so stunning it doesn't really need embellishing. But if you choose fabric in a solid color, you can use the ties, or the front wrap, to showcase decorative embroidery, machine stitching, beadwork or stencilling. Enjoy wearing your sarong with a matching top. Pair with a Timeless Top from Chapter Two, or Classic Blouse from Chapter Three, add a Cocoon jacket from Chapter Thirteen, and you have a dramatic suit.

Left: Sandwashed
silk cocoon
(Style #2) and
sarong with satin
acetate blouse
Right: Rayon print
cocoon (Style #1)
with purchased
blouse and pants

Chapter Thirteen

Cocoon Wrap

The last project in this collection is easy to create, stunning to wear, and proves once again the great success of a simple design. The cocoon wrap is the only garment in this book that has not been worn for centuries. When you see how easy it is to create a cocoon, you wonder why nobody thought of it hundreds of years ago. If you're looking for a good beginning project, this is it; you can serge, fuse, or sew it together in less than an hour.

PROJECTS

The photograph suggests the wonderful variety of looks you can create with the cocoon—everything from an art-to-wear top to an unusual jacket that can be paired with a skirt to create a suit. Style #1, a rayon print, can be closed with buttons or ties to create a top over leggings or pants. Style #2 is a sandwashed silk with contrast facing. Its longer lines make it useful as a jacket.

TIPS FOR PLANNING YOUR COCOON

The styles shown are constructed from the same simple pattern. This is a one-size-fits-almost-all pattern, suited for sizes 1–4 listed on page 3. If you're larger, make the pattern piece larger; if you're really petite, make it smaller.

A wide range of fabrics is suitable, but they have to drape well: cottons, cotton-polyester blends, silks, rayons, wools and wool blends, knits, and fleece. If you want to fuse your cocoon together, check the list of fusible fabrics on page 6. Avoid fabrics that have an obvious nap, diagonal design, or a plaid or other repeat that might be difficult to match. After you've made a cocoon or two, you can figure out ways to use fabrics with a nap or directional design. If you're using a wool, wool blend, or fake fur, you'll probably want to line your cocoon. You need the same amount of fabric for the lining.

If you enjoy painting on fabric, using decorative stitching, or adding any kind of embellishment, this is a wrap you'll enjoy creating again and again, for yourself or to give as a gift. The simple yet elegant and dramatic lines of the cocoon make it the perfect garment for showing off your creative ideas and handiwork.

WHAT TO BUY

◆ *Fabric:* This one-size-fits-almost-all garment requires 45" (1.1m)-wide fabric if you want a short sleeve, and 54–60" (1.4–1.5m)-wide fabric for a long sleeve. If you're lining the entire garment, buy the same amount of matching or contrasting fashion fabric as for the shell. If you're facing just the front, buy another 3/4 yd (61cm) of matching or contrasting fashion fabric for Style #1, and 1 yd (95cm) for Style #2.

Fabric Chart

	Short Sleeve	Long Sleeve
Fabric Width:	45" (1.1m)	54-60" (1.4-1.5m)
Style #1, Short	1.5 yds (1.4m)	1.5 yds (1.4m)
Style #2, Long	2 yds (1.9m)	2 yds (1.9m)

◆ *Patternmaking supplies:* Paper for pattern, measuring tape and pins, a ruler or straight edge, tailor's chalk or marking pens, pencil and eraser, and scissors.

- *Matching or contrasting thread* if you're sewing or serging
- *Purchased binding* for bound edges
- *Paper-backed fusible tape* if you're fusing Cocoon together.
- *Braid, trim or other decorative embellishments* you want to use.

PREPARE YOUR FABRIC

Follow instructions on page 5 to wash and dry, or dryclean, your fabric prior to cutting.

CREATE COCOON PATTERN AND CUT FABRIC

1 Choose the style you want to make.

2 Take your measurements to determine any adjustments you need. If you're in doubt, refer to the section on measuring on page 2 and on shaping fabric to fit you on page 7.

3 To create your pattern shapes, refer to the instructions in the section on patterns made of squares and rectangles, page 4. Also refer to the illustration Pattern Shapes for Cocoon, Styles #1 and #2. Adjust for your measurements.

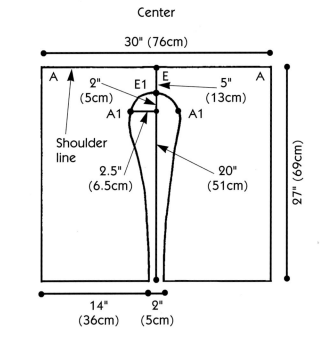

Facing, style #1

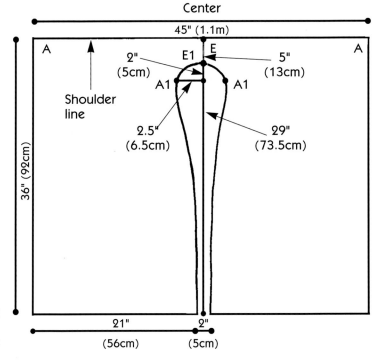

Facing, style #2

Pattern shapes for cocoon, styles #1 and #2

◆ • • ◆ **i d e a s** ◆ • • ◆

- Short on time? Choose a dramatic fabric. You'll be pleased with the effect without any extra embellishment, and you'll have a wrap or top in an hour.
- Add closures to the cocoon to create an unusual top to wear over leggings or a slim-line skirt.

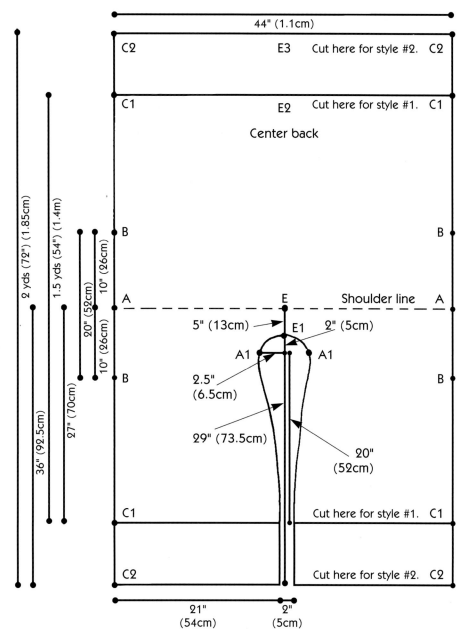

44" (1.1cm)

C2   E3   Cut here for style #2. C2

C1   E2   Cut here for style #1. C1

Center back

2 yds (72") (1.85cm)

1.5 yds (54") (1.4m)

20" (52cm)

10" (26cm)

10" (26cm)

27" (70cm)

36" (92.5cm)

B   B

A   E   Shoulder line A

5" (13cm) E1 2" (5cm)

A1   A1

2.5" (6.5cm)

B   B

29" (73.5cm)

20" (52cm)

C1   Cut here for style #1. C1

C2   Cut here for style #2. C2

21" (54cm)   2" (5cm)

Pattern shapes for cocoon, styles #1 and #2   Center front

4 Use the fabric layout in the illustration Fabric Layout for Cocoon, Styles #1 and #2. Pin the pattern shapes on the fabric as follows:

    a. Fold fabric in half lengthwise.

b. Fold pattern pieces in half lengthwise (along points E).

c. Place center front and back (points E) along fold of fabric.

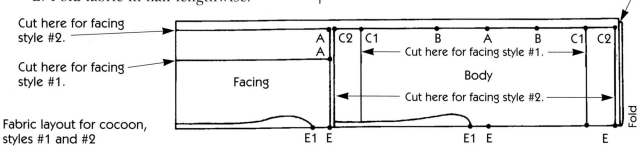

Cut here for facing style #2.

Cut here for facing style #1.

Selvages

A C2 C1   B   A   B C1 C2
A

Cut here for facing style #1.

Facing   Body

Cut here for facing style #2.

Fabric layout for cocoon, styles #1 and #2

E1 E   E1 E   E

Fold

5 Cut the fabric using scissors or rotary cutter and mat.

6 Mark alphabet points with tailor's chalk or fabric markers.

7 If you want a lined cocoon, cut lining to exactly the same measurements as fashion fabric shell.

CONSTRUCT YOUR UNLINED COCOON

Whether you sew, serge, or fuse your cocoon, use the following construction order. First, zigzag or serge all raw edges to finish and prevent fraying. If you're fusing, trim along the neck curve so it has a neat edge.

Finish neck and hem edge

1 If you're using a decorative binding, pin it in place around entire neck and hem edge, making ends meet along back edge of bottom. Sew or fuse in place.

2 If you're not using binding or facing, turn edges under 1/4" (6mm), press,

turn again 1/4" (6mm), press, and topstitch, slip-stitch, or fuse in place. See page 7 for more detailed fusing instructions.

Front Facing

1 If you're using a front facing, overlock or make a narrow hem on the side edges of facing [turn edges under 1/4" (6mm), press, turn again 1/4" (6mm), press, and topstitch, slip-stitch, or fuse in place].

2 Right sides together, sew facing to fashion fabric at neck edge and bottom hem edge.

3 Turn, trim, and press seam open, then press facing along edges.

4 Topstitch along shoulder from point A to point A so it looks like a yoke from the outside.

Style #2

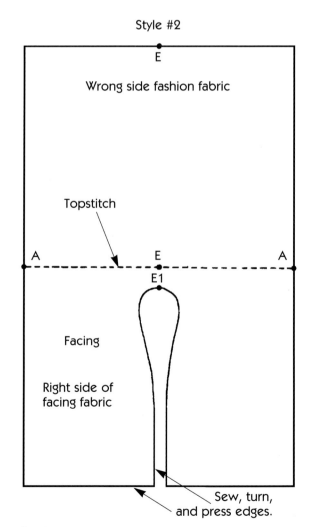

Style #1

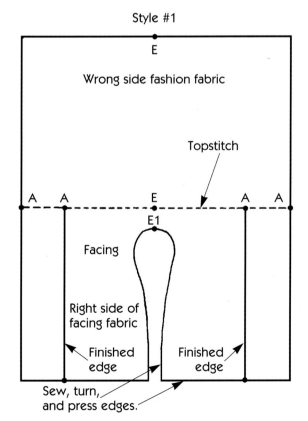

Facing cocoon front

Join side seams

1 Right sides together, fold along shoulder at points A.

2 Pin sides together from points B to points C.

3 Sew, serge, or fuse seam. (If facing extends to side seams, treat as one with garment.)

4 Press seam. Topstitch if you want.

Finish armholes

Finish armholes using one of these three methods:

◆ Sew or fuse purchased binding around armhole.

◆ Turn under 1/4" (6 mm), press, turn under another 1/4" (6mm) and glue or topstitch.

◆ Turn under edge 3/8" (1 cm), and fuse. Refer to page 7 for more detailed fusing instructions.

Hem

Sew:

Some portions of hem may already be finished (if you added a facing). If edge is unfinished, turn under 1/4" (6mm), press, turn under again 1/2" (1.3cm), press, and blindhem, hand-hem, or fuse in place.

Serge:

If edge has been serged, turn it under 1/2" (1.3cm) and blind-hem, topstitch, hand-hem, or fuse in place.

CONSTRUCT YOUR LINED COCOON

Attach lining

If you're lining your cocoon, follow the same steps to make both the cocoon shell and lining.

1 Join side seams.

2 If you're using a decorative binding, pin it in place around entire neck and hem edge, making ends meet along back edge of bottom. Sew or fuse in place.

3 Press entire edge of both cocoon and lining under 3/4" (1cm).

4 Pin the lining to cocoon shell, matching seams. Slip-stitch around all the edges of neck, front, bottom, and arm openings.

FINISHING TOUCHES

Add decorative touches to the finished cocoon around the neckline or on the facing or lining that cascades down the front. Add ribbon, frog, or interesting buttons and loops if you want to close it. It's ready to wear.

Pair the cocoon with Sure-Fit pants from Chapter Ten, the gathered skirt from Chapter Four, or the sarong skirt from Chapter Twelve, for an unusual, comfortable outfit.

Resources

BOOKS

Many Chilton books listed in the front of my book are excellent resources for embellishment and construction. I also like these books.

Sewing and Serging Basics

Complete Guide to Sewing, Reader's Digest, Pleasantville, NY, 1976.

Sewing Essentials, Cy DeCosse, Minnetonka, MN, 1984.

Sewing With An Overlock, Cy DeCosse, Minnetonka, MN, 1989.

Sewing With Knits, Cy DeCosse, Minnetonka, MN, 1992.

Simplicity's Simply the Best Sewing Book, New York, Harper Perennial, 1988.

Singer Sewing Step by Step, Cy DeCosse, Minnetonka, MN, 1990.

Vogue Sewing, Harper & Row, New York, NY, 1980.

Design Ideas

O'Connor, Kaori, **Creative Dressing**, Routledge & Kegan Paul Ltd, Boston, MA, 1981.

The Fiberarts Design Book II, Lark Books, Asheville, NC, 1983.

Thompson, Sue, **Decorative Dressmaking**, Rodale, Emmaus, PA, 1985.

Tilke, Max, **Costume Patterns and Designs**, Hastings House, New York, 1974.

Embellishment and Decoration

Avery, Virginia, **Quilts to Wear**, Charles Schribner's Sons, New York, 1987.

Complete Guide to Needlework, Reader's Digest Press, Pleasantville, NY, 1979.

Creative Sewing Ideas, Cy DeCosse, Minnetonka, MN, 1990.

101 Sewing Secrets, Cy DeCosse, Minnetonka, MN, 1990.

Holmes, Val, **The Machine Embroiderer's Workbook**, Batsford (c/o Trafalgar Square), North Pomfret, VT, 1991.

Meehan, Patricia, **Stencil Source Book**, North Light Books, Cincinnati, OH, 1993.

Moss, Kathleen, and Alice Scherer, **The New Beadwork**, Abrams, New York, 1991.

Newman, Thelma, **Quilting, Patchwork, Appliqué, and Trapunto**, Crown Publishers, New York, 1974.

Proctor, Richard M., and Jennifer F. Lew, **Surface Design for Fabric**, University of Washington Press, Spokane, WA, 1984.

Stitchery and Needle Lace From Threads Magazine, Taunton Press, Newton, CT, 1991.

Summer, Elyse, and Mike Summer, **Wearable Crafts**, Crown, New York, 1976.

Swift, Gay, **The Batsford Book of Embroidery Techniques**, Batsford, London, 1984

Wilson, Jean, **Joinings, Edges, and Trims**, Van Nostrand Reinhold, New York, 1983.

PERIODICALS

American Sewing Guild
P.O. Box 8476
Medford, OR 97504

Craft & Wear
P.O. Box 54494
Boulder, CO 80322-4494

Creative Machine Newsletter
P.O. Box 2634-PFF
Menlo Park, CA 94026

Creative Needle
Box 99
Lookout Mountain, TN 37350

Lace and Crafts
3201 East Lakeshore Dr.
Tallahassee, FL 32312-2034

Ornament
P.O. Box 2349
San Marcos, CA 92079-2349

Sew News
Sewing Update
Serger Update
News Plaza
P.O. Box 1790
Peoria, IL 61656

Surface Design
Association
P.O. Box 20799
Oakland, CA 94620

Threads
63 South Main Street
Newton, CT 06470

Wearable Crafts
P.O. Box 420235
Palm Coast, FL 32142

Are you interested in a quarterly newsletter about creative uses of the sewing machine and serger?

Write to:

The Creative Machine
PO Box 2634
Menlo Park, CA 94026-2634

Mail-Order Sources

Please ask your sewing-machine or fabric dealer to order you any product she or he doesn't stock. If you do not have access to a complete store, try mail order.

Aardvark Adventures
P.O. Box 2449
Livermore, CA 94551
(800/388-2687)
Unusual notions and tools

Bead Art
60 North Court Street
Athens, OH 45701
Beads, Fimo, beading supplies

BeadZip
2316 Sarah Lane
Falls Church, VA 22043
Unusual beads from around the world.

Cerulean Blue, Ltd.
P.O. Box 21168
Seattle, WA 98111
Procion dyes, fabric paint, SureStamp for making stencils, silk painting

Clotilde
2 Sew Smart Way
Stevens Point, WI 54481-8031
Special sewing machine feet, accessories, threads, fusibles, glues, much more

Craft Gallery
P.O. Box 145
Swampscott, MA 01907
Books and supplies for all genres of needlework

Dharma Trading Co,
P.O. Box 150916
San Rafael, CA 94915
(800/542-5227)
Fabric paint, silk painting, silk and cotton fabric blanks

Elsie's Exquisiques
P.O. Box 260
208 State Street
St. Joseph, MI 49085
Ribbons, rosettes, trim, tassels, fringe

G Street Fabrics
11854 Rockville Pike
Rockville, MD 20852
(301/231-8960)

Gardin' of Beadin'
P.O. Box 1535
Redway, CA 95560
Unusual beads, books, supplies

Global Village Imports
110 SW Washington #140
Portland, OR 97205
(503/236-9245)
Fabrics from South America, Mexico, Asia, Bali

Homespun Weavers
55 South Seventh Street
Emmaus, PA 18049
Lovely homespun fabrics

Kasuri Dyeworks
1959 Shattuck Ave.
Berkeley, CA 94709
(510/841-4509)
Unusual Japanese fabrics in cotton and silk

Keepsake Quilting
Dover Street, P.O. Box 1459
Meredith, NH 03253
(603/279-3351)
Everything for quilting. Lots of fabrics.

Lacis
1982 Adeline Street
Berkeley, CA 94703
Patterns, lace making supplies, sewing accessories

Lunn Fabrics
357 Santa Fe Dr.
Denver, CO 80223
(303/623-2710)

Michel Ferré Silks
P.O. Box 958
Niwot, CO 80544
Beautiful silks

National Thread and Supply Co.
695 Red Oak Road
Stockbridge, GA 30281
Threads and notions

Nancy's Notions, Ltd.
P.O. Box 683
Beaver Dam, WI
(800/765-0690)
Fabrics, threads, glues, fusibles, machine accessories

Sax Arts and Crafts
P.O. Box 51710
New Berlin, WI 53151-1710
Color catalog of everything for artists and crafters

Sew/Fit Co.
P.O. Box 397
Bedford Park, IL 60499
(800/547-4739)
Notions, cutting tools, and mats

Speed Stitch
3113-D Broadpoint Dr.
Harbor Heights, FL 33983
(800/874-4115)
Rayon threads and other machine-art supplies

Things Japanese
9805 NE 116th St., Suite 7160
Kirkland, WA 98034
Fabrics from Japan

YLI
P.O. Box 109
Provo, UT 84603-0109
Silk ribbon and unusual thread

Index

Adjust pattern, 4
Armhole, fuse, 19; shape, 8
Attach trims, 11

Balinese pants, 63
Beach towel, styles from, 16, 52, 69
Belt, 10
Bias tape, 12
Boat neck, 5
Bodice: Drop-waist, 36;
  Easy waist, 34; Empire, 34;
  to shape, 9, 37

Caftan Robe & Dress, 45+
Calculating size, 3
Child's: dress, 34; gown, 41;
  kimono, 69; vest, 59
Classic Blouse & Turtleneck Top, 21+
Clip-and-Curve Method, 7
Cloak, 51
Closures, vest, 60
Coat, evening, 69; winter, 51;
  with scarf, 52
Casing, 10, 30
Cocoon Wrap, 81+
Cocoon, lined, 85; unlined, 84
Create pattern, 4
Cut pattern, 4

Double tucks, 8
Dress, 33+

*Easiest Winter Coat & Summer
  Wrap,* 51+
Edgestitching, 12
Elastic corded gathering tape, 10;
  see also elastic gathering tape
Elastic gathering tape, 10, 30, 42, 49
Embellish garments, 10 – 13
Empire bodice, 34

Fabric, fuse, 6; prepare, 5;
  preshrink, 5
Fabric glue, 6
Fabric list for fusing, 6
Facing neckline, 48
Fit, 3, 7; crotch in pants, 65
Fuse, how to, 6;
  Clip-and-Curve Method, 7, 60;
  Seam-Fusing Method, 7

Fuse armhole openings, 19;
  curves, 18; neck edge, 54, 60;
  neckline, 7; seams, 7;
  side slits, 19; trims, 11
Fusible fabrics, 6
Fusible tape, 6, 7, 11

Gathered Skirt, 27+
Gathering tape, 42;
  see also elastic gathering tape
Glue, fabric 6, 11
Glue trim, how to, 11, 19
Gown, *see Swirling Gown*

Jumper, 33
Kenzle, Linda Fry, 11, 58

Kimono Coat, 69+
Kimono, lined, 73; unlined, 72

Large-sized figure, 40, 45, 57

Maternity dress, 34
Measurements, 2
Measurements form, 3
Miyake, Issey, 7

Neck edge with scarf, 55
Neckline, how to:
  add facing to, 48; fuse, 7;
  trim, 42
Neckline shapes, 5
Nightgown, 39; child's, 41

One-Hour Vest, 57+
Overlock, 12, 13;
  see also Serging tips

Pants measurements, 64
Pants, Balinese, 63; palazzo, 63;
  Sure-Fit, 63
Paper-backed fusible tape, 11;
  see also fusible tape
Pattern, paper for, 4
Pockets, 31, 64, 66
Preshrink fabric, 5

Raincape, 52
Robe, 45

Round neck, 5
Ruana, 52

Sarong Skirt,, 75+
Sash, 16, 73
Scam allowance, 4
Seam-Fusing Method, 7, 19
Selecting trims, 11
Serging tips, 18, 21, 24
Shaeffer, Claire, 64
Shaping, 3, 7 – 10
Shape: armhole, 8, 9; bodice, 9, 10,
  42; bustline, 10; hip, 9; sleeve, 8;
  shoulder-bustline, 9, 37, 61;
  waist, 9
Shorts, walking, 63
Shoulder-bustline tucks, 9
Simplest Dress & Jumper, 33+
Side closures, 60
Side slits, fuse, 19
Single tucks, 8
Size Chart, 3
Skirts: broomstick, 27; dropped-
  waist, 28; gathered, 27; sarong, 75;
  slim, 28; straight, 27; tiered, 28
Slit-collar neckline, 5
Square neck, 5
Stocksdale, Joy, 63
Straighten fabric, 5
Summer caftan and dress, 46
Summer wrap, 52
Supplies, 2
Sure-Fit Pants & Shorts, 63+
Swirling Gown, 39+

Timeless Tops 15+
Topstitching, 12
Trims, 10 – 13
Trim neck edge, 42
Tucks, 8, 9; trimming, 61
Turtleneck top, 21

U-neck, 5

V-neck, 5
Vests, 57+

Waistband and casing, 30
Waistband ties for pants, 66;
  for sarong skirt, 78
Wrap, cocoon, 81; summer, 51